THE FIFTH GOSPEL

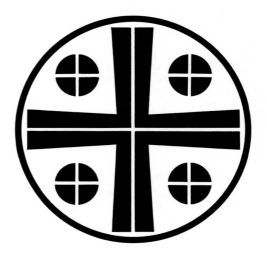

A parable is a story or a series of images which can be understood on more than one level. There is a message offered beyond the literal meaning of the words themselves. Jesus spoke often in parables and tells His reason in the Gospels: "And He said, Unto you it is given to know the mysteries of the kingdom of God: but to others in parables; that seeing, they might not see, and hearing, they might not understand." (Luke 8:10) It seems more than appropriate to incorporate this idea into a book about Jesus. The "you" in the above quotation refers to the disciples, so let the reader who is willing to give energy and time toward the understanding of the work be likened to a disciple, and let everyone else who picks up "The Fifth Gospel" be "the others."

The structure of a parable gives in return for the thought devoted to it. If one is satisfied with the mere dramatic value of the story, that is good and sufficient...the parable has given some pleasure. But if one seeks to link the story to a symbolic meaning, the potential is there. The photographs for this book are in essence the same. The viewer can be satisfied with the simple visual imagery of things in the Holy Land or he can approach the work with a desire to discover the hidden poem in each picture. The captions are an attempt to push the door of that second level of understanding slightly ajar, as well as create a mood in which to approach the pictures... the rest is up to the reader.

ADVISORY COMMITTEE

Archbishop George Appleton, Anglican Church
Dean Harold Adkins, Anglican Church
Bishop Norair Boyharian, Armenian Church
Dr. Sahak Ralaybgian, Armenian Church
Reverend Dr. Robert Lindsey, Baptist Church
Reverend Albert Dale Truscott, Evangelist Church

THE FIFTH GOSPEL

A Parable about the land of Christ
as photographed by Elliott Faye,
described by Fr. Godfrey Kloetzli and
edited by Fr. Ignazio Mancini
who wrote the preface and epilogue
Parables by Laura Faye Taxel
Designed by Asher Oron

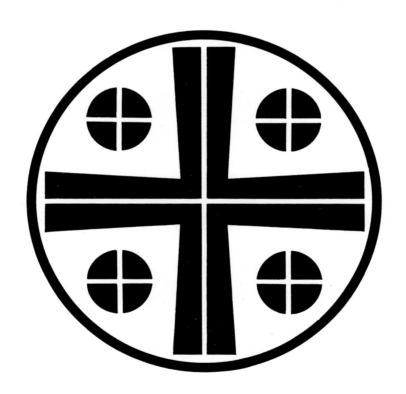

Prentice-Hall, Inc., Englewood Cliffs, N.J.

Library of Congress Cataloging in Publication Data

Faye, Elliott.
The fifth gospel.
1. Jesus Christ — Biography — Devotional literature.
2. Palestine — Description and travel. I. Kloetzli,
Godfrey. II. Title.
BT306.5.F3813   232.9'01   72–7267
ISBN 0–13–314344–9

© 1972 for first English edition published by
Prentice-Hall, Inc., Englewood Cliffs, N.J.

Aerial Photomosaic by
The Photogrammetric Engineering Co. Ltd., Tel Aviv

Old Maps of the Holy Land
from the collection of the National Library,
Hebrew University of Jerusalem.

© 1972 by Bibleland Publications Ltd., Tel Aviv

Produced by Massada Press Ltd., Jerusalem

Printed in Israel by Peli Printing Works Ltd.

CONTENTS

PREFACE

"For whatever was writen in former days was writen for our instruction, that by steadfastness and by the encouragement of the scriptures we might have hope." (Romans 15:4)

I find the title of this book, "The Fifth Gospel", particularly pleasing, especially as the concept is that of Ernest Renan, an author who certainly could not be accused of clericalism. Indeed the Holy Places, like the Four Gospels, have the unique power to help us know Christ better and to place us in the presence of the mystery of His life and His death.

We hear a good deal of talk these days about returning to our sources, tracing the path back to the Church as it was in its beginnings. Reading the Bible is once more held in high esteem. The historical figure of Christ, effaced by time, disfigured by a criticism scientific only in appearance, and often mystified by pious souls, is now revealed to us again with clearly defined features and more accurate reference to His time and geographical environment. It is clear that our generation is closer to the Christ of the first Christians of the Church of Jerusalem, many of whom must have known and listened to Him.

We need to resist the temptation to disregard the living person of Christ and devote ourselves solely to Christian values, which are excellent in themselves but, devoid of the person of Christ, are emptied of what constitutes their real force—since it remains always true that the eyes want to see and the hands to touch. The woman who had had an issue of blood elbowed her way through the throng, in order to touch the border of Jesus' garment. Zacchaeus climbed up into a sycamore to see Him pass. Thomas insisted that he wanted to put his finger into the wounds of the nails.

Awaiting their own resurrection, the Saints rest in the shadow of Christ's humanity. Christian mysticism is different from other mysticisms precisely on this point. In other forms of mysticism, the soul loses itself in God without a human intermediary, but in Christian mysticism, as a rule, the soul passes through the humanity of Jesus to reach God.

Whoever loves Christ as He is presented by the Evangelists can never sunder himself from the Holy Places. He carries them always with him because the events of His life are imprinted on their stones.

The purpose of this richly illustrated volume is to provide an introduction to the Holy Places for those unable to visit them and to keep those pilgrims who have had the happiness of visiting them from ever forgetting the only visible traces left on earth of Jesus Christ, Who at Nazareth became our brother, a member of our species; Who was revealed in Bethlehem to display His mildness and humanity; and Who, in Jerusalem, gave the supreme proof of His love for mankind by dying for their redemption.

Turning the pages of this book the reader will feel that he is following in the steps of Jesus. He goes everywhere with Him: to Nazareth, to Bethlehem, along the banks of the Jordan, to the shore of the Sea of Gennesaret, to Capernaum, to Tabgha, up the Mount of Beatitudes, up Mount Tabor, to Bethany, to the Cenacle, to Gethsemane, along the Via Dolorosa, to Calvary, to the Sepulchre, to Emmaus, and to the Mount of Olives.

The reader of The Fifth Gospel will learn for himself the truth of Châteaubriand's words that the Holy Land is the only country on earth which reminds the traveler of things both human and heavenly, and which, precisely because of these associations, arouses impressions and thoughts in the depths of the soul which no other place inspires.

Everyone has something within himself which connects him to the Holy Land and all may find themselves anew when they visit it. Because for three years Christ and His Apostles wandered over its white dusty roads; because He knew its pure dawns when, at daybreak, the sky takes on an innocent tenderness. From this place, from this dim atom, He saw the heavens declare His glory. The heavens opened to Him in Bethlehem and followed Him constantly thereafter until they were darkened on the day of His death.

It is my heartfelt wish that this book may contribute to acquainting men with Christ and with Him Who sent Him.

Fr. Ignazio Mancini, OFM

INTRODUCTION

"...not that there is another gospel... For I would have you know, brethern, that the gospel which was preached by me is not man's gospel."
(Galatians 1:7, 11)

hy yet another book on the Holy Land? The title is itself an explanation. By studying the "Fifth Gospel," the land of Christ, we can more clearly understand and appreciate the Four Gospels of the New Testament. The most effective way to learn the "Fifth Gospel" is to actually visit the Holy Land and read Matthew, Mark, Luke, and John at the traditional sites of the events described by them.

For a number of years it has been my great privilege to lead pilgrims through the Holy Land. They have come from every corner of the globe and have been of every walk of life. Clergy and laity, young and old, learned and simple — all have expressed one thought after their visit, namely, that now they would be able to read their Bible with far greater insight and understanding than ever before.

It is inspiring to see young students, self-assured in their knowledge, as the young tend to be, stunned into silence as they visit the sacred sites; it is moving to witness the deep humility of great scholars at the same sites. I have many warm memories of the effect of the Holy Land on pilgrims. Two of them I would like to share with you. The first took place on a late autumn day. With a group of visitors I boarded an excursion launch to cross the Sea of Galilee. After we had been under way only a short time, a sudden storm arose. The boat pitched wildly, large waves broke over the bow, and the passengers huddled in fear in the lower cabin. Some of the women began to weep and anxious faces turned to me. I took out my New Testament and began to read aloud from St. Matthew 8:24—26, "And behold, there arose a great storm on the sea, so that the boat was being swamped by the waves; but He was asleep. And they went and woke Him, saying, 'Save us, Lord, we are perishing.' And He said to them, 'Why are you afraid, O men of little faith?' Then He rose and rebuked the winds and the sea; and there was a great calm."
I could see the light of understanding replace the fear in their eyes, and, strangely enough, when we reached the shore the sea was again calm and serene. This group had shared the terror of the Apostles and had felt the comfort of the realization of God's presence.

The second event took place on a beautiful spring day on the Mount of the Beatitudes. Among the group that day was a dear old pastor. I asked him if he would like to read the Sermon on the Mount to us. He was delighted. As he read, a great peace fell upon us all. When he came to the words, "Look at the birds of the air...Consider the lilies of the field..." he stopped, and we were all suddenly very conscious of the fields around us ablaze with wild flowers of every color, while the sound of a multitude of birds filled the air with their song. The old pastor's eyes filled with tears; blindly he held out the New Testament for me to finish. Never again will anyone who was present that day read the words of the Sermon without reliving that moment.

This is what we mean by the "Fifth Gospel": the land of Christ as it was and as it is today, as it can be experienced by every Christian.

We must begin by setting the stage, as it were, for the great drama that was played out so long ago. There are three backdrops for the scenes: the geographical, political, and religious atmospheres of the Gospels.

The Geographical Setting Physically the Holy Land is a very small portion of the earth. Its length from Dan to Beersheba, the ancient boundaries, is about 350 kilometers. In width it varies from some 40 kilometers in the north to about 135 in the south. But small as it is, it possesses a great variety of landscape. Deserts and fertile plains, mountains and valleys, rivers and lakes are all to be found there. In a short time one can travel from lush fields and groves to an inferno of blasted crags and ravines, blazing deserts of rock and stone — a portion of the land seemingly cursed by God.

The physical aspect of the land today is much as it was in the time of Christ. The land can be divided into parallel zones running north and south. On the west we find the seacoast and the verdant plain of Sharon. In ancient days the prophet Isaiah praised its wealth and beauty, and in present-day Israel it presents a panorama of abundant groves and fruitful fields. Then there is a soft line of hills and a second alluvial plain. In this plain, wheat grows extremely well. In Christ's day it was known as the Shephelah.

Passing on to the east, we find the country rising by three steep steps, cut by deep narrow gorges, to the high country forming the backbone of the land. It must be borne in mind that when I speak of "high" country and of mountains it is only by comparison with the rest of the country. In many other lands these mountains would only be called hills. Mount Merom, the highest mountain in Israel, is only some 1,300 meters in height.

This backbone of the land was divided into three zones. The southern area, called Judea, was and is on the whole an arid land, a fitting background for the ancient Jews and their capital, Jerusalem: It required determined men to carve a living out of those hills, just as it required determined men to remain faithful to their God and His Temple. It is a land with a golden brown color, like the tawny hide of the Lion of Judah. Farther north one comes to the central portion, Samaria. Here the landscape is more varied. It is a softer land, with stretches of rich valleys between its hills. In the time of Christ this was the land of the Samaritans, those people disdained by the Jews as heretics. On Mount Gerizim the Samaritans had built their temple to rival the one in Jerusalem, causing enmity between the two peoples. For this reason Jews traveling between Judea and Galilee first went down to Jericho, crossed the Jordan, and then proceeded northward through Perea.

Finally, to the north we come to Galilee, the third section. This is a land of many hills and plains, a well-watered and prosperous land. Even today it is the most delightful part of the country, a gentle and easy-going place. With the plain of Esdraelon sweeping eastward from the Mediterranean, one is in a region far different from all the rest of the country. In Galilee starts what is known to geologists as the Great Rift, a great slash in the face of the earth stretching from the foot of Mount Hermon, down through the Red Sea, and on into the heart of Africa. It is astonishingly deep and comparatively narrow, never more than 19 or 20 kilometers from east to west. This rift in the crust of the earth, the deepest on the face of the planet, grows wilder and more desolate as it goes southward, relieved only by a few beautiful oases, Jericho being the richest. The Sea of Galilee with its sparkling fresh water, filled with fish and girded by luxuriant fields and prosperous settlements, marks the north of the rift. At the southern end lies the Dead Sea, surrounded by gaunt cliffs and deserts and reeking of sulphur and other chemicals, truly a place of despair. Yet both of these seas receive their water from the same source, the Jordan River. Wherein lies the difference? For every drop the Galilee receives from the Jordan, it gives up as much or more. Yet the Dead Sea, like a miser, greedily holds on to every drop that it gets. Perhaps we have here yet another illustration of Our Lord's teaching that it is more blessed to give than to receive.

The Political Scene The Hasmonean royal house, which had risen with Simeon Maccabeus, had been weakened by internal strife and finally fell before the armies of Pompey, who had decided to add Syria, and thus Judea, to the Roman Empire. Pompey appointed Hyrcanus II, heir of the Hasmonean house, as high priest and ethnarch. When hostilities broke out between Pompey and Julius Caesar, Hyrcanus and his adviser, Antipater, sided with Caesar. Following Caesar's victory Hyrcanus was confirmed in the offices of high priest and ethnarch, and Antigonus, the rival claimant, was rejected.

After the assassination of Caesar and during the subsequent civil war, chaos swept the land. Antigonus proclaimed himself king. As a counter-measure, Mark Anthony and Octavian, the future Augustus, conferred the crown of Judea on Antipater's son, Herod. After a bloody war Antigonus was defeated and executed and Herod strengthened his claim to the throne by marrying Mariamne, the granddaughter of Hyrcanus II. An able and wily king, Herod held onto and enlarged his kingdom until his death in 4 B.C. His court was of the utmost magnificence and his building activities were equally majestic. On the seacoast he built the splendid city of Caesarea, which became the country's largest seaport. He rebuilt Samaria on a grand scale, giving it the Greek name Sebaste in honor of Octavian, the Augustus. His mighty palace fortresses of Massada and Herodion still bear witness today to their original magnificence and luxury. Jerusalem was enriched with palaces, new walls and towers, a theater and stadium, and other public works. The Temple was rebuilt on a plan of unparalleled splendor.

Despite all his accomplishments, Herod degenerated into a monster, murdering kinsman and stranger, friend and foe. His beloved wife was murdered, a tragic victim of his paranoia, as were some of his sons and a host of others. It was this same Herod who ordered the Massacre of the Innocents and was thus the cause of the flight of the Holy Family into Egypt. On his death the kingdom was divided among three surviving sons. Archelaus received Judea, Samaria, and Idumea; Herod Antipas, Galilee and Perea; and the third son, Philip, the northeastern regions of Trachonitis, Batanea, and Auranitis. All three were given the title of ethnarch. In A.D. 6, after ten years of rule characterized by great severity, Archelaus was removed by Augustus, and his domains came under direct Roman rule as a single province commonly called Judea; in control of the lands was a Roman procurator, who was, in turn, subordinate to the Roman governor in Syria. Although the Romans ruled with a firm hand, they allowed the people a good deal of freedom in their personal affairs and religion, always with the understanding, however, that there be no thought of resisting Rome. It was the procurator who was responsible for collecting revenue for the Empire and keeping the peace in his domains. The fifth procurator was Pontius Pilate, who ruled Judea from A.D. 26 to 36 and who condemned Our Saviour to death.

The Religious Scene With the disappearance of the Jewish kings of Judea, supreme authority was vested in the High Priest. He was assisted by the Sanhedrin, the high court of the Jews, and by doctors in religious law. The Sanhedrin was made up of seventy judges, including priests and Levites. Also prominent were the scribes, although they were a separate group, representative of the Pharisee sages. When the High Priest attended a meeting of the Sanhedrin, he officiated as president. Of course the Temple at Jerusalem was the supreme place of prayer, and it was the only place of sacrifice. Synagogues existed throughout the country, but these were centers of prayer and instruction.

The Law was the heart and soul of the religion of the Jews, but there had grown up religious sects which fought bitterly over its interpretation. The major sects were the Pharisees and the Sadducees. These two groups had come into being because of the problem of how the Jews were to live in the midst of a pagan world.

At the time of Christ the Sadducees drew their numbers mainly from the wealthier classes. They were high officials, rich merchants and landowners, and members of the old royal families. They believed only in the Law as it was written and rejected the oral Law. A problem not specifically dealt with in the written Law, they felt, should be acted upon according to the requirements of the time. They were also firm believers in the doctrine that man should aspire to well-being in this world and not look to the next. Man must make the choice between good and evil, for God, Who was above all such things, took no notice of them. Since the Sadducees were the party of the priests and guardians of the Temple, they had great influence in both religious and political life. And as they had control of the Temple treasury, they had great economic power. The High Priest was, naturally, a Sadducee.

The Pharisees, on the other hand, insisted that the Law had to direct man's every action. Therefore it was necessary to complete the written Law with tradition, the oral Law. Ever since the return from the Babylonian exile, the oral Law had been continually formulated by the scribes and applied to every detail of daily life.

While the Jewish kingdom had been expanding under the Maccabees, the Sadducees had exerted great influence, but with the gradual subjugation of the land, the Pharisees had gained the ascendancy. At the time of Christ the Pharisees had the greater influence on Jewish life, and their interpretation of the Law dominated the political and religious spheres. They maintained themselves as a group set apart, keeping ritually pure and avoiding contact with the common people, although continuing to live among them. Their way of life demanded complete dedication to each and every detail of the Law, not only strict purity in the matters of food and clothing but close attention to the hundreds of injunctions regarding daily life. Fidelity to the Law became increasingly important to the Pharisees, and it was this dedication that eventually made possible the reorganization of Judaism after the destruction of the Temple.

Thus we have sketched the background for the great drama of the Four Gospels. It is the aim of this book to provide for you as clear a picture as possible of their setting as it was and as it is today in an endeavor to help you increase your knowledge, understanding, and love of the Word of God.

ERRA

CARMEL

Jokncan

CANAN

Shimron
meron

Nazaret

Dor

Taanach

M

Æ

PEREZ

OCCIDENT

Tappuah

Forte hic
ZEMA =

Sheche
VAL

Zemaram

Tirzah

Lasharon

Makedah

Bethel

Gibeon

Japho

Gezer

3

AMORHÆI

H

Jeru

Sepultrum Rachelis

Moriath
mons

Bethleh

Gath

Hepher

Adullam

Libnah

Ekron

Gedor

SA

Ashdod

Jarmu

Hebron

Lac

LISTEI

EVM

NAZARETH

"And he went down with them and came to Nazareth, and was obedient to them; ...and increased in wisdom and in stature, and in favour with God and man."
(Luke 2:51–52)

an anything good come out of Nazareth?" (John 1:46). And if, as we may suppose, such was the opinion of many of Jesus' contemporaries, one cannot help wondering why it was in Nazareth of all places that Jesus spent the greater portion of His Life. What was so significant about Nazareth that there He could prepare Himself for His public life? The answer is simply *nothing*. Nazareth was a completely insignificant town. It is never referred to in the Old Testament. Even the Jewish historian Josephus does not mention it among the 204 villages and towns he lists in his description of Galilee. All we know is that, as St. Matthew tells us, "He [Joseph] went and dwelt in a city called Nazareth, that what was spoken by the prophets might be fulfilled, 'He shall be called a Nazarene'" (Matthew 2:23).

Not that much is known of His boyhood. The Gospels are silent about it. All we know is that He grew up not in the courts of the Temple amid the scholars and teachers but in a carpenter's shop in a poor, mean town, amid simple craftsmen and shopkeepers not so very different from the folk of Nazareth today. In the words of George Adam Smith, the great geographer of the Holy Land, "the value of a vision of the Holy Land is that it fills in the silences." Through the Nazareth of today, we can reach back to the little town of two thousand years ago.

Nazareth now is a busy place: Lacking the serenity of Bethlehem, it is full of hustle and bustle, cars and buses, donkeys and carts. The town is the center for the Arabs of Galilee and their largest market. The streets are lined with cafes and shops, with many small woodcarvers and carpenters to recall the trade that perhaps Jesus learned.

Yet nothing could be more uplifting to the pilgrim than his arrival at Nazareth. Coming from the south he crosses the fruitful and beautiful plain of Esdraelon, following the road as it twists and winds up through young forests until, cresting the hill, he finds the town spread out at his feet in a natural hilltop amphitheater.

This is the little town where Mary lived, where Joseph, her husband, worked at his trade, and where the Archangel Gabriel brought her his wondrous tidings. In this town Jesus lived some thirty years with His mother and foster-father and was "obedient unto them" (Luke 2:51). The great Via Maris, the thriving highway running between Egypt and the nations of the North and East, passed at that time but a short distance from Nazareth. Thronged with pilgrims and merchants, it swept across the plain of Esdraelon, near the foot of the hill upon which Nazareth is nestled. To the north ran the highway between Acre and the Greek cities of the East,

along which legions marched, princes paraded with their retinues, and travelers of all sorts journeyed. How many people must have passed along those two roads without an inkling that the Light of the World lay hidden so close!

Entering the town we find at its heart the great Basilica of the Annunciation. New and modern, the structure nevertheless has carefully preserved all that is old. Although much has yet to be finished in the way of decoration, the great basilica is substantially complete. It consists of two churches, the lower and the upper, harmonizing the old and the new. The Upper Church, a brilliant, modern concept, has walls decorated with mosaic panels presented by the communities of nations all over the world; the Lower Church, dark and shadowy, lit only by flashes of color from the small side windows, cradles like a precious jewel the ancient grotto. Here in the grotto the angel Gabriel came to Mary and she said to him, "Let it be done to me according to your word" (Luke 1:38). Today this precious grotto, all that is left of Mary's home, is enshrined in the very heart of the Basilica of the Annunciation.

This church is the latest in a long series of shrines that have stood on this spot since the end of the first or the beginning of the second century when the first followers of Christ, the Judeo-Christians, created a house-church here. During the excavations of the area, many graffiti were uncovered, and their references to Mary and the Annunciation have shown that the building was indeed a religious structure. A few fragmentary remains of that church can still be seen.

With the arrival of Constantine there arose a magnificent basilica. Pillars which formed part of its structure cluster today around and in front of the grotto in the Lower Church, together with the remains of the southern wall and the apse.

Constantine's shrine survived the Persian invasion of the seventh century when Chosroes and his destructive hordes bypassed Galilee. In succeeding centuries, however, it fell into inglorious ruin. In the twelfth century that great and good man, Tancred, Crusader Prince of Galilee, undertook its restoration, and a new gothic-style cathedral arose, worked on, as were so many churches of that era, by an army of patient craftsmen. But not for long was it destined to stand to the glory of God. In 1263 it was destroyed utterly by the cruel Sultan Beibars. That same tyrant had the Christians of Nazareth mercilessly butchered when they refused to embrace Islam.

Only a few walls remain of Tancred's church, but excavations for the present building uncovered five beautiful capitals which had been prepared for the structure but never put into position. In the new basilica they form the background to one of the side altars in the Lower Church.

After Tancred's cathedral was decimated, a series of small chapels arose, each in turn destroyed, until in 1730 during the space of only seven months a larger church was built which survived until it was removed to make way for the present basilica. From the middle of the fourteenth century the Franciscans struggled and died in their attempts to preserve this sacred spot. Driven away time after time, they always returned. Now in this great new church, they see the fulfillment of centuries of dreams.

Beyond the Basilica of the Annunciation stands another modern church, that of St. Joseph, marking the traditional site of the carpentry shop, today a cave scooped out of the living rock beneath the church.

A few hundred yards north of the town center, at the side of the main highway, is the spring that, until very recently, was the sole source of the town's water supply. Here Jesus must often have come to draw water for His mother. To reach the spring we pass through the lovely Greek Orthodox church that is over the site and go down the small stairway, then along the passage lined by ancient marble, worn smooth by the hands and bodies of countless thousands of pilgrims. The Greeks believed that it was here at the well that the archangel first appeared to Mary, and, frightened she ran home where Gabriel came to her again with his wondrous announcement.

Nearer the town center the Greek Catholic church marks the site of an ancient structure traditionally believed to have been the synagogue attended by Jesus. St. Luke tells us of the day when Jesus taught in this synagogue, and in explaining a passage from the prophet Isaiah He so angered His fellow townsmen that they seized Him and "led Him to the brow of the hill on which their city was built, that they might throw Him down headlong. But passing through the midst of them He went away" (Luke 4:16—30). The traditional site of this hillbrow is a steep, wooded mount, located a little to the east of the road to Afula and known as the "Mount of the Leap of the Lord."

There is an ancient legend in connection with this event, according to which Mary, hearing of what was happening, rushed out, as any mother would, to go to her Son's aid. Halfway to the precipice she saw the townspeople returning without Jesus and was seized with a tremor of fear. Today a Poor Clare Convent, known as the Tremore, stands on the spot.

Strip away the accretions and distractions of modern Nazareth, and here, again, we reach out to the simple, humble home of the Holy Family.

If a man passes by a doorway which is dark and silent, is there reason to stop there? But if a man passes by a doorway from which pours forth light and music, is he not drawn to enter and be fortified? Before the time of Jesus, Nazareth was a dark and silent doorway, a poor village from which issued no promise for a wanderer. But since the time of His boyhood there, Nazareth and the Church of the Annunciation have welcomed an unending procession of pilgrims from all over world. For the memory of His youth has become light and music. Nazareth is a beckoning doorway.

In old Hebrew, Nazareth is called Netzer, meaning germ or shoot, indicative of its insignificance among the cities of the land. But the shoot has grown into a mighty tree. The name of the city that once could be forgotten as soon as it was out of sight, now lives like the memory of a festive scene in the minds of all who pass.

18

We cannot know a flower when it is only a small seed in the palm of the hand. The child Jesus was but a seed and none could know what manner of blossom would emerge. He grew from baby to boy, caught, as are all little boys, among the flurry of women's skirts, the murmur of women's voices. In those unknown years He was any-boy, every-boy, playing, learning, eating, sleeping amidst the smell of bread and the taste of milk.

But mysterious ties attached this any-boy to things greater than Nazareth. He was imperceptibly different, necessarily alone. His mission cast a shadow that clung to Him as He grew in mind and body, the mission growing as well, until the shadow drew the faceless boy away from the shelter of anonymity, outward on the path of prophecy.

The boy Jesus lived with the rhythm of everyday tasks. A mother's errand or the eye's delight must often have carried him to the marketplace where a shiny bead, some simple household tool, or a bit of gaily colored cloth were among the treasures to be found. He must have passed regularly by the stalls where necessity and pleasure joined together and clothed themselves in carnival costume.

Each successive generation goads a land and its customs to change. Old things become new and different things appear to fulfill the demands of desire's voice. Yet what is altered retains forever a whisper of what was. The marketplace of Nazareth, crowded with new and tempting wares, is an image of the world of Jesus, different, yes, but somehow the same.

Jesus was bound to earth as well as to Heaven, the Son of Man and the Son of God. A carpenter and a virgin, a son of Bethlehem and a daughter of Nazareth, were chosen to be the guardians of His youth.

Matthew has written of Joseph that he was visited by an angel, who told him that his betrothed had conceived a child by the Holy Spirit. The angel asked Joseph to name the child Jesus, meaning Saviour. Joseph, being a good and godly man, did as the angel had asked.

Luke has written of Mary that she was visited by the Archangel Gabriel, who told her that she would give birth to the Son of the Most High.

"And Mary said, 'Behold the handmaid of the Lord; Be it unto me according to thy word.' And the angel departed from her."   *Luke 1 : 38*

When a young girl peers into a mirror, she sees, perhaps, only a reflection of herself. Or, she may see the chin of her father, the smile of her mother, the nose of her uncle, or the eyes of her grandmother.

So it is when the world today looks into the face of a young girl. It may see only the girl, or it may see many girls. It may see Mary, filled with joy and wonder, growing in a way that is unchangeable in a changing world.

The eyes of a young girl are like a drop of seawater that reveals both itself and the whole of the sea. These eyes of humble female youth sing of their own spring and of all springs past. Young girl eyes tell the story of Mary; of those not-yet-woman eyes that looked out upon her Galilee world her Nazareth day.

The girl Mary was espoused to Joseph, boy become workingman, who was moved by a will that is greater than the understanding of men. He took the girl forward, out of her sheltered past, to emerge the predestined Mother.

In AD 337, the first Christian church was built in Nazareth. For centuries to follow, churches were built, destroyed, and rebuilt. Today, twenty-three churches and many monasteries and convents enshrine the holy places of Nazareth. The city is dedicated to preserving the memory of Mary, Joseph, and Jesus and their Nazareth life. Small chapels and massive stone churches open their doors to the devout and welcome the visitor. Bells ring loud and sonorous, chiming an invitation to Christian pilgrims from the world over. Red-robed priests, hooded monks, and black-draped nuns mingle with tourists and Arab residents. Once an unimportant little village known only as a stopping place for merchants from the East, Nazareth today is among the foremost Christian cities in the Holy Land.

SYRIÆ
PARS
Scham olim
Damascus
Vallis Hermon
Daria
Emathitæ
Zoba   Tibebath   FIURÆA
BASAN   Argol   Baalag
Adai   Baalgat   Phiala fons
REGNUM
Fordanis fluuis   Copar
Gaulana   Gamela
Arama   Cedar   TERRA   HUS.
Cefarea   Philippi   Seleuua   TRACHONITIS   GERASÆORUM
nunc Helle   na   REGIO   Astaroth REGIO
Dan   fons
For fions   Enhazor   Jordanis fluui   Corazaim
Bethanatha   Adama   Iuliada
Bethfemes   Lekum
Rama   Hazeroth   Tri   bg. Ahion   Caldes
Edrai   Meroth   Iereon   Capharnaum
CHA   Hamath NANÆI.   Asnoth   Neptalim
Racoth   Affor vel Hefron   Hinaffach
GA   nunc   Antiopia   Kaman
Rehuc   Charian
GALILEA   Haroreth   LI
Hamon   Horma   SUPERIOR SEU   Zepht
Berithus   Spelea   GENTI   Bethlem
Cana   Ifaly   Sidimzer   Cabul
Nsar flu.   Belei   Ncupha   Capharath
T.Rama   fort   Ebron   Bethmek
Cananea   Thoron Ty   Abelena   Gifgala
Sidon   beris olim   Reguin caftr.
Saws n.   Aefaph
Antilibanus   Betza   Tribus After   Salron
mons   Amna   Naafon
Sarepta   Cukeffa   Montforr   Selama
Fons hortorum   Hoffa   Mafal
C.Blanco   Scandaria   Amead   Vallis Ieph
PHOE   NI: thael
Indi   Zabulon
Fons aquarum   Affur   Bethdagon
viuentium   S.Georgy
Tyrus   Scandalium   Amead
Sur nunc   Soron vel
S. Lamperti

Mo. Arnon
Care
PHILAD
Philadelphia
Rabbaath

Ifie hodie multa et ruinofa
habitacula vifuntur, fed
deferta et nominibus carétia.

Mons Galaad
Rama
Theman   Bathen æi
Geray   Mahanaim
Ecbatana   Manæi
Afteroth   Carnay
Maffbath   Iabis   PineL
Datheman   Tubbin
Bara   Caffbor   Maffha
Galaad
Labis   Gadera
Pella   Ephraim
Pella
Gadara   Araboth
Ammaus toparchia
Mare Galilææ vel   Debir   Mageth
Tiberiadis quod   Dion
Tarichea   et Stagnù Gene=   Ammaus
Iefferkin   zareth
Genna   Arbel
bar   Therme
Magdalum   Thabes
Thenee
Abel   Hippon   Enaber
Betfaida Iulias   Genefareth   Bethoma   Belvoir   Bethfan
Dothaim flu.   cha   Bethmanu   Scythopolis
Gabaroth   tha   Belliforf
Fatapata   Belina   Amathuntha   Magnus
Bethulia   Tubavia
Dothaim   Thabor mons   Endor   A.
ElKofi   Abelina   Chelma   Kifion
Ablon   Kanathon   Gadara
Tribus Zabu   Naim   Adremmõ
lon   Buria   Faba
Rama   HEVÆI   Darabitta
Charta   Azechim   Apher
GALILEA   Nazareth   INFERIOR
Sephor   Mefhra   Pherefæi
Cana Galilea   Iaknoam   Gahaa
CBA   Sihor   Chifon torrens   Hippon
Sepulchrum   Narbathæ toparch i
Memnonis   Cain   Aret
M. Carmelus
Ifa
Castrum Pere
grinorum, olim
Dora

Ptolemais
Acon

Mare   Syriacum

MARIS   MEDITER   RANEI

SEPTENTRIO

Horæ itineris   1 2 3 4 5 6 7 8 9 10
Miliaria Germanica   1 2 3 4 5 6 7

GALILEE

"…Jesus came into Galilee, preaching the gospel of God, and saying, 'The time is fulfilled, and the kingdom of God is at hand; repent, and believe in the gospel.'"
(Mark 1:16–17)

alilee, the northern third of the Holy Land, was in Our Lord's time, as it still is, the most beautiful part of the country. As are Nazareth and the environs of the Sea of Galilee, so are the forested mountains and fertile valleys of Galilee studded with sacred sites, like so many precious pearls, each a jewel to be treasured.

First there is Cana, situated a short distance northeast of Nazareth. Like Nazareth it was a small, unimportant village. One of its inhabitants was Nathaniel bar Tolmai, to whom, as we read in the first chapter of St. John's Gospel, Philip came to announce that he had found Him of whom Moses and the prophets had written and that His name was Jesus of Nazareth. At the sound of the name, Nathaniel voiced the widely-held opinion of Nazareth and asked, "Can anything good come out of Nazareth?" Nevertheless he went with Philip to Jesus, Who, when He saw him approaching, cried, "Behold an Israelite indeed in whom is no guile!" Thus Nathaniel joined the little band and later was chosen to be one of the twelve. Today he is better known by the name of Bartholomew, derived from his surname, bar Tolmai, the son of Tolmai. His home is traditionally believed to have been on the site of the present Greek Catholic church.

It was in Cana one day that a marriage was about to take place. Among the guests were Our Lord's mother and Jesus Himself with some of His disciples. We all are familiar with the story of what happened at that wedding. There was a domestic crisis when the supply of wine ran out. Mary, as any good housekeeper would, noticed the commotion behind the scenes and went to her Son, asking that He do something. Jesus at first demurred. The time, He said, had not yet come for Him to begin His public ministry. But Mary seemed insistent, and summoning the servants, she told them to obey His orders.

Why was Mary so insistent? One explanation I once heard was that Mary understood that when Jesus performed this first miracle of His public ministry, she would lose Him from her home, for henceforth He would belong to all mankind. It is worth noting that, although Mary is mentioned afterward as having been present on various occasions, not another word of hers is quoted. When she spoke to the servants at the marriage feast, she was speaking to us all. She had raised Him and cared for Him since His birth; now she was presenting Him to us. And the words she spoke, the last of hers that are recorded, are addressed not only to the servants, but to you and me as well: "Do whatever He tells you" (John 2:5).

Today the Latin parish church stands on the site of an ancient shrine that marked the traditional site of that first miracle. There is a fourth-century mosaic in the church, with a Hebrew inscription of which part can still be read: "In happy memory: Joseph, son of Tanhum, son of Butah, and his children, who made this table [altar]. May blessings be to them. Amen." A converted Jew by the name of Count Joseph of Tiberias had been commissioned by the Emperor Constantine to build shrines at a number of the lesser holy sites: Sepphoris, Tiberias, Capernaum, and Cana. It is quite within reason to assume that the church inscription refers to that Joseph and is evidence that this is indeed the site of the first miracle.

Leaving Cana for Tiberias, to the northeast, we pass through the Valley of Turna, where the Apostles, being hungry one Sabbath, plucked the ears of wheat to eat (Matthew 12:1-8).

North and slightly to the west of Nazareth is the site of the ancient town of Sepphoris, traditional home of St. Joachim, the father of the Virgin Mary. Tradition has it that Mary spent her girlhood here before being betrothed to her cousin Joseph of Nazareth. A church was built in Sepphoris by Count Joseph in the fourth century and restored in the twelfth, but today only a small fragment remains. There is also an orphanage for girls there, a particularly appropriate location for such an institution.

To the east of Nazareth the symmetrical dome of Mount Tabor rises up to heaven, as one author has it, "like an altar that the Creator built to Himself." This is a mountain that has always had a special significance. Here, in Old Testament days, Deborah assembled the warriors of Israel under Barak and watched them sweep down to destroy the Canaanite army of Sisera. To this mountain Our Lord brought His Apostles, and leaving nine of them at its foot, took Peter, James, and John up with Him to the top, to be witnesses to the Transfiguration. As Peter and the others watched in terror, two figures appeared and talked with Jesus; a cloud covered the mountain-top, "And a voice came out of the cloud, saying, 'This is my Son, my Chosen, listen to Him!'" (Luke 9:35). The same behest His mother had uttered at Cana. When Peter saw the radiant figures of Moses and Elijah standing with Jesus, he was overcome with emotion and offered to erect three tabernacles—one for each of them. Symbolically, the new basilica on Mount Tabor fulfills this desire, for while the main part of the church is dedicated to Jesus, the chapels in the bases of the two towers are dedicated to Moses and Elijah respectively. This modern church is built upon the ruins of a Crusader structure which, in turn, rests upon the remains of a fourth-century shrine. The actual Crusader altar is still in use in the lower level of the modern church.

Just as the Sea of Galilee can be called God's sea, this mountain is surely God's mountain. Standing on the summit of Tabor, looking out over the land in which Our Lord carried out His Galilean ministry, we experience such peace and tranquillity as can only come from a sense of the nearness of God.

To the east of the foot of Mount Tabor stands Endor, where King Saul, upon dabbling in the forbidden witchcraft, suffered his dark night of despair, only to learn that he and his sons must perish in the battle of Gilboa to be fought on the morrow. And away to the south and east is the site of the ancient city of Beth Shean, from whose ancient walls the headless body of Saul was hung until it was rescued by his followers.

South of Mount Tabor stands the little town of Nain, known today as Nein, where Our Lord performed one of the most touching of His miracles, raising from the dead the only son of a widow and restoring him to her.

Across the southern part of Galilee stretches the rich and fertile plain of Esdraelon, coveted and fought over by so many peoples throughout the ages. At its southern end, near the pass through which the ancient Via Maris stretched, stood the mighty city of Megiddo. Here archeologists have uncovered no less than twenty successive settlements or cities, the first one built more than 6,000 years ago. The armies of all the great empires marched past this site: the Egyptians, the Assyrians, the Persians, the Greeks and the Romans, the might of Saladin and of Napoleon, the armies of Turkey and Britain—all have gathered and many have fought here. After so many battles the hill of Megiddo, Har Megiddo in Hebrew, seems a fitting place for the last battle between the forces of good and evil that will be fought before the Day of Judgment, when the kings of the earth "will be gathered to the battle of that great day...into a place called in the Hebrew tongue Armageddon" (Revelation 16:14, 16).

Eastward, along the hills that mark the southern rim of the plain of Esdraelon, we come to the town of Jenin, standing on the old borderline between Galilee and Samaria. This was the place where Jesus cured the ten lepers, of whom only one, a despised Samaritan, showed any gratitude by returning to render thanks and glory to God.

Even though Samaria has never been a part of Galilee, we can say something about it here, for Our Lord must have traveled through it several times on His way to and from Jerusalem. The hill of Samaria stands about halfway between Nazareth and Jerusalem. It was here about 928 B.C. that the mighty king Omri built the new capital of the Northern Kingdom of Israel and gave it the name Samaria.

Under his son, Ahab, Samaria developed into a great and rich city with fine palaces and a "house of ivory" (I Kings 22:39), whose existence was borne out by the discovery of beautiful carved ivory inlay panels during the excavations of Ahab's city. Also uncovered was a walled basin which recalls the pool in which Ahab's blood was washed from his chariot after his death, as Elijah had foretold (1 Kings 21:22).

Ahab had married Jezebel, a princess of Phoenicia and priestess of Baal, and she introduced Baal's pagan worship into Israel, thereby making a bitter enemy of the prophet Elijah. Following Ahab's death in battle, the commander of his army, Jehu, rebelled against the family of Ahab. As Jehu advanced, Jezebel learned of his coming and "painted her eyes and adorned her head and looked out of the window. And as Jehu entered the gate...he lifted up his face to the window and said, 'Who is on my side? Who?' and two or three eunuchs looked out at him. He said, "Throw her down." So they threw her down and the wall was sprinkled with her blood, and the hoofs of the horses trod upon her" (II Kings 9:30-33). Thus died the wicked queen Jezebel.

The downfall of the kingdom of Israel came with the Assyrian capture of Samaria, after which the

Israelite tribes were scattered and lost. Later Herod rebuilt the city in a magnificent, grandiose style, renaming it Sebaste, Greek for the name of his patron, Augustus. It was here, according to an ancient tradition, that John the Baptist was buried, although differing traditions have him imprisoned and beheaded in Herod's new palace in Tiberias or in the desert castle of Machaerus. In the fourth century a basilica was built in Sebaste over the traditional site of John's tomb, and 800 years later the Crusaders replaced it with a cathedral considered in its day one of the most beautiful structures of the century. Its remains still stand, now converted into a mosque, and its guardians show to visitors the rock-cut tomb where, they say, John was imprisoned and later buried. To Sebaste, too, came Peter and John after the first converts to Christianity had been made, in order to lay their hands upon them and bestow upon them the Holy Ghost.

Nearby, a little to the east, is the city of Nablus. This modern name is derived from the Greek Flavia Neapolis, given it in honor of Flavius Vespasian, when the old city of Shechem was rebuilt after the war against Rome. Shechem itself, which lay a little below the present site of Nablus, was a very ancient town. Abraham built an altar to God there, and Jacob purchased a field from Hemor the She-

chemite and dug there the deep well known still by his name. When Joshua arrived he held a general assembly of the twelve tribes in the valley in which Shechem was situated, with Mount Ebal on one side and Mount Gerizim on the other. There they performed the ceremony of the curses and blessings, as prescribed by Moses (Joshua 8:30-35). Turning first to Mount Ebal, on which six of the tribes were drawn up, the Levites recited aloud, one after the other, the curses pronounced by the great lawgiver (Deuteronomy 27:11-26). And after each anathema the people answered, "Amen." Then, turning toward Gerizim, they pronounced the blessings, the people repeating "Amen" each time.

It was to the well of Jacob that one day Our Lord came with His disciples on the way from Jerusalem to Galilee. Jesus was weary and sat down to rest while the disciples went on into the town to fetch Him some food. Then a woman of Samaria came to draw water and Jesus said to her, "Give me to drink" and there followed the beautiful story told in the Gospel of John (Chapter 4). To pause here and drink the water from Jacob's Well and read again the account of those events of long ago, is to be refreshed indeed, in both body and spirit.

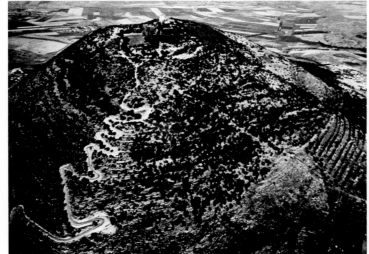

Most men choose some corner of the land and call that place their home. Jesus claimed no plot of land His own. He lived among the people, beside the trees, upon the grass. Any Galilee stone may have pillowed His head, any leafy branch given shelter to Him. The Galilee was His courtyard, and all the land His house. With neither plow nor gold did He lay hold of His estate. Yet He was not without a home for His home was boundless.

A time came when Jesus' first community was not large enough to hold His message. He needed wide and rolling spaces so that the sound of His Word could sail across the land and reach a hundred thousand ears. He chose the Galilee for the home of His ministry as a man would choose a wife. For the Galilee, it is said, is a feminine province; it is womanland —rich, fertile, and fruitful. The land offered up its bounty to Him who gave of Himself so freely. He ate olives from her trees and bread baked from her grain. He nourished the people and the land nourished Him. Woman is a receiver, and like woman, the land of the Galilee received the Kingdom which He proclaimed. So with a ceremony of miracles, Jesus bound himself to this province.

In searching for a favorable place to take root, many men chose the region of the Galilee. They found the land there welcoming and compliant. The ground was fecund, the water in good supply, and the weather warm and gentle. Houses were built, children were born, and villages grew. Men labored hard and reaped the fruits of their labors. And the land rested quietly beneath men's hands. When Jesus began His ministry in the Galilee, nine cities surrounded the lake and many other cities and villages sprawled atop the hills or clustered upon the Plain of Esdraelon. The land had been tamed. The soil was well-farmed, the area well-populated. The lake was filled with fish and boats. Many roads criss-crossed the district. There could be no better place for The Teacher to reach the people.

To Galilee, to the Gal-lilies of the field, all around the
Galilee, the ministry of Jesus made itself known. He gave life
in Nain; He healed the deaf on the bounds of Decapolis; He
sighed for mankind in Dalmanutha, and found His church
in Caesarea-Philippi.

As yeast makes dough to swell, so His reputation caused
His following to grow larger. And numbered among the
believers were many women: Mary of Magdala, Joanna,
Susanna.

Some of these Galilee towns are homes yet today, while
others breathe no more. But each name carries with it a memory,
and each place guides the seeker through the land in the
manner of an arrow on which are emblazoned the words
"He Was Here."

At a wedding in the valley village of Cana, the first bond was forged between the Son of Man and the Galilean land.

A bride comes to her groom as a girl, the miracle of her womanhood not yet revealed.

A groom comes to his bride as a boy, the miracle of his manhood not yet disclosed.

On the marriage day, girl becomes woman and boy becomes man, and their future begins to unfold.

Jesus entered Cana as all other wedding guests, His power not yet revealed. He joined in the marriage festivities, His Purpose not yet disclosed.

But amidst the dance, the song, and the celebration, Jesus revealed His power and disclosed a small measure of His birthright. He made wine from water, and quiet Cana sang with the music of the first miracle.

A marriage, a marriage! Old women and aging men are joyous and remember their own youth.

A marriage, a marriage! Young men and girls feel their blood run merry and are warmed by images of their own wedding day to come.

A marriage, a marriage! Children, mothers, fathers, grandparents, friends, and kin all join together to celebrate the cycle that means the continuance of generations.

The wedding clothes, the wedding food, and the wedding guests coax the day to last forever. The wedding song, the wedding dance, the wedding wine call a welcome to the future. In all the world, there is no more glad hour than the hour of a wedding.

Long after the first miracle had been performed, when His
reputation had grown and His name was spoken with awe,
Jesus came once again to Cana. He had been to Jerusalem and
was returning to the bosom of the Galilee. As He passed by
Cana, a nobleman whose son lay ill in distant Capernaum
begged Jesus to make the boy healthy again. Jesus cured the
ailing child without journeying to Capernaum, and from that
time on, the nobleman and all his household were followers of
Jesus, for they had been given a Sign.

The land unfurls at the foot of the mountain. This is the plain of Esdraelon and the mount of Tabor. The fields of the plain are those fields that spread their green and brown furrows under the gaze of Jesus, James, Peter, and John. For after He had spoken much, healed many, and traveled great distances, Jesus sought to meditate in silence. And tradition holds that the solitude He chose was upon Mount Tabor. A fertile, yielding land He must have seen from this place of prayer.

But the mountain became the seat of something greater than prayer. Moses and Elijah descended to Jesus, and in the Transfiguration of which Mark and Luke have written, His body and His clothing became as much spirit as their spirits. Overcome with awe, Peter spoke of constructing three tabernacles. And on this holy site, men raised glorious churches to heaven and other men razed them to dust. And new churches were built, and again men destroyed them. Again and again this happened, in the manner of men.

When He came down from the mountain into the farmland, a multitude greeted Him anew. And another man begged Him to heal yet another child. For also in the manner of men, the people desired much. Neither He nor His disciples spoke to the people about what had happened on the mountain.

If we were to ask the sky, "What breed of bird wings across your face?" the sky would answer, "All."

If we were to ask the soil, "What sort of growth springs from your entrails?" the soil would answer, "All."

And if we were to ask history, "What mold of man and what manner of woman was beloved by Jesus?" history would answer, "All."

Poor and wealthy, ill and well, to each He gave a promise or a sign. Young and tender women served Him as they would have served a husband. Strong and fiery men were his apostles of peace. Mothers and fathers, surrounded by children of their own, became His children. Embittered elders forgot the harshness of their lives and spread the sweet News of His Message and His Miracles.

He woke a buried hope. And when men and women felt the living hope stir within their hearts, they believed and became His followers.

Cæsarea Palestinæ
Ptolom...
Turris stratonis
Carmel
Bel...
Gaba
na...
Besor
Betha...
Antipatris
Dora
Sabulon
Saron
Naamata
Nara bata
Bethlemes
Teconan
Aialon
Adaria
Madrem
Sarid
Carmeli valles
Iosue
Bethe ron
mon
Nazareth
Seperis Dio...
Lachis
Sepulchri
Madrem
Aphec
Naim
Mons Tabor
Tamnathsera
Adadrem
EPHRAIM
Esdrelon
Suna
SABULON
Ciriat Iearmi
Gaser Sichem
Samaria
Ieireel
Betulia
Mispha
Gibeon
Lebna
MANASSE
Isas
Giabera
ENIAMIN
Silo
Thirta
HAR
Dabereth
Goron Beta
Gibea
Ennon
Gelboe
Ietopata
Rama
Bethel
Tiberias
Cineret
Anatoch
Hai
Ephren
Gasrafes
Sahari
Palm
Debora
Arbela
Zela
Zena
Abelmen
Ramath
Ensemes
Almath
Ephra
Tapuah
Zalemni
Cison
Iericho
Irnini
Iordanes
Iherus
Ennon
Betabara
Gilgal
Bet hlan
Fons heliei Betaula
Zartan
Tisga
Paul.
Nahu naim
Zittim
Deser
Debir
Ephron Ophra
Bethabara
Libais
Acib.
Hu Mortuus
GAD
Helbon
Tesbe
Relenor
Neb. Morses
Hispa
Carnar
Lili
Carnath
Flumen Tella
Iopa
Ramath in Gilead
Belmeon
Sabama
Te Pe
Madian
Aroer
Iaier
RUBEN
Nephat
Neda be
Zeb
Arta
Ra
Engallim
Luith
Horonaim
Diblat baim
Cademoth
AMMON
Fons Elim
Arnon
Mathana
Betonim
Hennith
Dibongad
Desertum
Cademoth
Desertum

Tyrus

Biblium

Aziba

Mърна

Berithus

Achtaph

Terra Syro Phænicia

Terra Gibili tarum

Elmelech ca Camala

Gibiliten

Rama

Canana

Mons Liban

Cujaala

Aphec

ASER

Alcath

Bezeeh

Hemath

Betemec

Abran

Hileph

Hat

Rohob

Mons

Paneas

Cabul

Hazon

Cenereth

Mons

Fons J.

Abdon

Jordanis

NaaBan

Vallis Senium

Fons

Sephet

Cedes Nep

talim

Mazaleth

Cæsaria Philippi

Carthan

Abelmaacha

Nephtalim

NEPTALIM

Riblath

Arach

Aseroth

Machati

Bethsaida

Caphernaum

Maron

GALILEE

Sweta

co

ralim

Gaulon

Seleucia

BASAN

Geluri

REGNUM

Astaroth

Bosra

Heli

Cedar

Gerata

Gamala

Hermon et Senir et Senes

Camon

Calphar

Mons

TRACONITIS

Terra Aram

Jabes

Zoba

Terra

TERRA

Regnum Zoba

Gilead

Galaad

Mons Galaad

Dara

Hippon

Tibenth

Terra Tob

Iudicum

CELESYRI

Carnaim

Sdra

 Um Vinctorum

SEA OF GALILEE

"And passing along the Sea of Galilee, he saw Simon and Andrew the brother of Simon casting a net into the sea... And Jesus said to them, 'Follow me...'" (Mark 1:16–17)

here is a charming old Jewish legend that after God had created the seven seas of the world, He created the Sea of Galilee for His own pleasure. Standing on the shores of that lovely body of water, or better still, viewing it from a distant height, it is easy to appreciate that story. Nestled within its surrounding hills, the sea —in fact it is a sweet-water lake—is ever changing, ever beautiful, a fitting setting for so many of Our Lord's wondrous works.

Here, dawn breaks over a misty, mysterious scene, spreading a golden haze over serene, rippling water, shadowed by the encircling hills. Most days of the year the sun shines forth from a blue, almost cloudless sky and is mirrored in the tranquil, azure waters of the lake. The western shores are lined with the green of fields, plantations, and woods; on the far side the barer eastern hills give back the sunshine in a golden light slowly transformed through shades of rose to the purple hues of evening and night.

But there are days when the lake reflects no such serene enchantment. When the tempest roars and the rain slashes down, the sea churns in answering fury, tossing the fishing boats like playthings, and tearing at the shore. I have seen a strong stone pier reduced overnight to rubble, boats wrecked, fields flooded and their crops ruined. No wonder the Apostles were turned by a storm into cringing children, crying out to Jesus to save them lest they perish!

The waters Our Lord stilled shimmer now under sunshine or moonlight. He well knew the villages, the cities, and the countryside on all the shores of Lake Galilee. On the northern shore, with the lake stretched out before it, stands Capernaum, the town He loved and where He made His home after He left Nazareth.

Today there is little enough to be seen, but when Jesus chose Capernaum as his home, it was an important town, standing on the great highway—the Via Maris—that ran from Babylon to Egypt. From the New Testament we can deduce that the town possessed a customs-house and was garrisoned by at least one hundred soldiers. But not only would the local people hear His message. The constant stream of travelers passing through the town would also learn of it and carry His new teaching far and wide. That is how the report of Jesus' words and deeds spread, so that people knew Him when He appeared in other towns and other people made the journey to Galilee to see and hear the wonderful new teacher.

Just below Capernaum, in a beautiful little cove surrounded on three sides by gently rising hills, the people crowded around Jesus, anxious to hear Him better but in fact nearly pushing Him into the sea.

So He climbed into a fishing boat and, putting off a little from the shore, found the perfect position from which to address the multitude. Fishermen still come here to sort their catch and mend their nets after a night's fishing and, watching them, it is easy for us to remember that Jesus walked one morning by the sea and, looking at much the same scene, uttered those fateful words: "Come, follow me, and I will make you fishers of men" (Matthew 4: 19). Peter, Andrew, James, and John left their nets and followed Him.

Not far from the cove is a flat stretch of land covered for most of the year by a green carpet of grass. There, one evening, some five thousand men, women, and children sat down and were fed by Jesus with five loaves and two fishes. Jesus had spent the night in prayer and meditation with His disciples on the hilltop. In the morning, looking over the lake, He spoke to them those marvelous words of the Sermon on the Mount, after which the world could never be quite the same.

The jewel of the towns that gird the lake was in Jesus' time, as it is today, Tiberias. Built by Herod Antipas during Jesus' childhood, Tiberias was a splendid place of palaces and public buildings adorned with columns and shining with the finest marble. On a hill above the city stood Herod's own palace, agleam with brilliant mosaics of glass and gold representing both men and beasts. To pious Jews, however, such pictures were a violation of Divine Law and an affront to God. The palace was an abomination. The city, too, was considered unclean, for it had been built over a cemetery and the houses themselves stood upon the tombs of the dead in further disregard of the Law. Accordingly, no good Jew would enter the city and we can be sure that Our Lord never did so.

Within a century, however, a new city of Tiberias, rebuilt about a mile to the north after the mass destruction of the war with Rome, was to become one of the four holy cities of the Jews, as it was here that the Mishnah and Palestinian Talmud were completed.

Above Tiberias, a little to the north, rise the heights of Arbel where battle after battle has been fought over the centuries. There the armies of Herod the Great subdued the people of Arbel after their premature rebellion against Rome. From these heights above the lake, the people flung themselves to their deaths rather than submit. Nearby, a dozen centuries later, Saracens and Crusaders met in the battle that spelled the end of the Crusader kingdom of Jerusalem. Northward again is Wadi Amud, a deep winding cleft, gouged out by earthquake and floodwater.

This is an area so full of history that diligent treasure-hunters can find flint blades from the Neolithic Age, pottery of the Bronze Age, Roman and Byzantine coins, glass, and fragments of mosaics. And below, beside the shimmering waters of the lake, is the site of Magdala, birthplace of Mary of Magdala. In Jesus' time this was an important fishing and fish-drying town, but little remains today. The eye turns rather to the fertile plain of Gennesaret, from which the lake takes one of its names, where tall date palms sway above the bright green of fields and plantations. In this beautiful stretch of land, the ancient Jews were known to say, the gates of paradise were hidden.

A little further on, at the crest of a small hill, there comes into view the site of the first multiplication of the loaves and fishes and the Mount of the Beatitudes. At the foot of this hill on the shoreline is the Chapel of the Primacy where Our Lord first appeared to His Apostles in Galilee after His resurrection from the dead. This chapel is a peaceful place, and sitting on the nearby ancient steps used by the fishermen of long ago, we can almost see Christ standing there that morning, calling out to His beloved friends who had been fishing vainly all night. After they had caught the great draught of fish at His command, they came ashore and found some breakfast already prepared for them. Then His questions to Peter, three times asking him if he loved Him; and with each of Peter's affirmative answers Christ gave him the mandate: first "Feed my lambs," again "Feed my lambs," finally "Feed my sheep."

From this spot it is exhilarating to walk the two kilometers to Capernaum, knowing that Jesus Himself so often walked this way. In fact the road must follow nearly the very route of the old Via Maris. What thoughts pass through our minds as we stroll where His feet trod, seeing what He saw? As this part of the Holy Land is also below sea-level, it is very hot a good part of the year. Therefore, as He passed this way, Our Blessed Lord often felt tired and thirsty. It is a spiritual gift to feel the same as we follow in His footsteps. We can sense more fully His humanity and realize more clearly that He did not move through this world dissociated from earthly things, but that He felt the heat of the day, that His feet and legs would be weary at the end of a long day's trudge, that His eyes would ache from the burning glare of the sun, that He would be hungry and thirsty. And yet, as we so often read, He never let any of these things stop Him from continuing His work when those who were sick and those who wanted to hear His words came to Him.

Finally we arrive at Capernaum. Once so populous and important, there is nothing here now except the small Franciscan house and a few ruins. Prominent among these are the remains of the synagogue, built about A.D. 200 on the site thought to be that of the synagogue in which Christ taught. There are also other ruins which, under the patient hands of the archeologist, are slowly emerging from the soil which has covered them for so many centuries. These excavations began just a few years ago as the result of removing for repair a Byzantine mosaic from the floor of a small church. The church was built over what was then believed to be the house of St. Peter. Once the mosaic had been lifted out the opportunity was taken to explore below the site. The entire area was found to be covered with the ruins of houses of the first century. One of the houses was located immediately beneath the Byzantine church, and it was found that in the first century this house had been converted into a house-church by the Judeo-Christians, the first converts to Christianity. Without going into detail regarding the excavations, it may be said that the archeologists are convinced that this is indeed the house of Peter and probably the very house in which Our Lord lived during His sojourn in Capernaum. As one steps over the doorsill of this house one is awed by the knowledge that the foot of Jesus most likely trod on this very stone!

It was here in Capernaum that Christ worked so many of His miracles. In the synagogue He cured the man possessed of the evil spirit. The same day He cured Peter's mother-in-law, and "Now when the sun was setting, all those that had any that were sick with various diseases brought them to Him; and He laid His hands on every one of them and healed them. And demons also came out of many, crying, 'You are the Son of God!' But He rebuked them and would not allow them to speak, because they knew He was the Christ" (Luke 4:40-41). And it was while He was walking somewhere near the town that the woman with issue of blood touched the hem of His garment hoping thus to be cured. Near here, too, the Centurion met Him as He was on His way to that good man's house to cure his servant; and the Centurion spoke those words still so often used today, "I am not worthy to have you come under my roof; therefore I did not presume to come to you. But say the word, let my servant be healed" (Luke 7:6-7). And He also went into the house of Jairus, the ruler of the synagogue, and raised his daughter from the dead. Here, too, He cured the man with the withered hand, and the paralytic who had to be let down to Him through a hole in the roof because of the great crowd around the house in which He was. And it was in Capernaum that one day He called to Levi, who was working in the customs-house. "And he rose and followed Him" (Mark 2:14); thus did the future Evangelist, Matthew, join the disciples of Our Lord. And it was here in the synagogue, after the second multiplication of loaves and fishes, that He promised the people to give them His own body to be their food. It was here He had Peter catch the fish and remove the tax money from its mouth. Coming here to Capernaum from the far side of the lake where He had performed the second multiplication of loaves and fishes, He walked upon the water.

Today, in this place, there is a sense of His presence. As a Methodist minister said to me as we sat in the ruins of the synagogue late one afternoon, "If Jesus and some of His disciples were to walk past me now, I wouldn't feel surprised."

Another joy to be experienced here is the sunset, which is especially beautiful in the autumn. Sitting on the northern shore one watches the sun drop behind the hills to the west. It grows darker and darker around you and then suddenly there is a burst of rose and gold in the sky. The hills turn a soft red and the sea and sky blend into a marvelous mixture of the palest pinks and purples and soft, luminescent gold. For a moment the very earth seems to hold its breath at the sheer beauty of creation, and then, all too soon, it is over and night quickly falls.

Near sunset one day a storm was brewing over the lake. High above was that wonderful pink sky.

On either side of the lake some clouds were trailing long silvery drapes of rain, forming a frame, as it were, for a billowing black cloud that was advancing to the center of the lake. From the depths of this cloud rumbled deep, yet oddly soft, thunder, while flashes of lightning lit up the folds of the cloud. I had been showing the lake to a small group of people and we all stood awestruck, careless of the few drops of rain that had begun to fall. Then someone said in a quiet voice, paraphrasing Matthew 17:5, "And He spoke to them from a cloud."

There are other sites we may visit in Galilee. Three kilometers to the north of Capernaum are the ruins of the town of Chorazin, while about the same distance to the east is the site of Bethsaida. These two cities shared with Capernaum the anger of Our Lord for here, too, He was rejected. "Woe to you, Chorazin! Woe to you, Bethsaida! for if the mighty works done in you had been done in Tyre and Sidon, they would have repented long ago in sackcloth and ashes. But I tell, it shall be more tolerable on the day of judgment for Tyre and Sidon than for you" (Matthew 11:21-24).

Here, from the heights above the northern shore, we can also turn and gaze at the whole length of the Sea of Galilee: Down on our right are the tall hotels, the cafes, the beaches of Tiberias with their motor boats and water skiers, and the white passenger boat plying across the lake to where kibbutz Ein Gev makes a welcome patch of green on the eastern shore; at the far end, the tall palm trees cluster around the point where the Jordan flows southward out of the lake.

This is the Sea of Galilee that "God created for Himself" and the towns and countryside Jesus knew and loved. Surely a lifetime could be spent absorbing the spiritual messages of this area. Like everyone who comes here, we want to linger but few of us are able to do so.

At dawn, when the sun has not yet risen, the fishermen go
out in their boats, drop their anchors, and cast their nets.
Silently and patiently they wait for the fish. And by the time
the sun is high and the air hot, the fishermen's boats are home
again. The nets are alive and aglitter with the silver-scaled
bodies of catfish, carp, and St. Peter's fish. It has always been
like this with the fishermen of the Galilee. A fisherman's day
has always been long, his work strenuous. Boats must be
caulked and painted afresh. Nets must be untangled and
repaired. The catch must be separated, cleaned, and sold. Fish
to trade for a sack of grain, fish for a chowder, or modern-day
fish to be frozen and stored—it is all the same. Fish for a
livelihood—a man's labor in exchange for his life.

Woman is not always calm or gentle. Nor is sea. Peaceful waters that invite men and their vessels can suddenly become wild and raging. The Kinnereth was calm when Jesus and His disciples set forth, but during their journey a great storm arose.

Fear is like a parasite that may bore its way into the best of fruits. Fear of the storm ate its way into the faith of the Apostles, and in their terror they awakened the sleeping Jesus. He restored tranquility among the disciples, as tranquility was restored to the sea. The Apostles were rebuked and their faith renewed, and the sea was once again as it had been.

The heart is slow to accept new truths and faith is sometimes long in coming. His disciples were like open coffers to which Jesus proffered the riches of His teaching, yet none too swiftly did they accept the treasure as their own.

It was evening and the disciples were once again on a boat at sea. A great wind suddenly swelled the waves and churned the waters, and rowing was very difficult. Jesus stood alone on the far shore and saw His disciples struggling. It is written in Matthew's Gospel that He went to them, walking on the water. But they knew not what they saw and were frightened.

A great crowd followed Jesus into a lonely place. Empty and unpeopled land suddenly bore the pressure of many feet. And it is written that from five loaves of barley bread and two fishes, Jesus made food enough to still the hunger of the multitude.

Five thousand were fed and logic does not explain it. Five thousand were fed with a handful of food and only faith in God can justify it. For the world is fraught with events that cannot be understood by the mind alone but require also some sense of the divine.

By word of mouth, the memory of this miraculous event was passed from man to man throughout the land. By Gospel word, the story has passed from place to place and time to time. And by the Word which rises silently, immemorially from the land that was party to the wonder, the event is preserved from generation to generation.

The land and its people were waiting for the Word. On a hill on the shores of the lake of Galilee, Jesus poured out such words as were never heard before. They were like a heady wine, strong and intoxicating. The men who heard them came from many parts of the land—from the north and the south, the east and the west. They had left their homes, their fields, and their boats.

The land, too, was a witness, and today the land alone remains as a witness of that day. The domed church is surrounded by the ancient stones that seem to be ever listening to the eternal Sermon of the Son of Man.

Today the beauty contained in His teaching is mirrored in the beauty of the countryside, the pure and simple cadence of the Beatitudes reflected in the pure and simple curves of the land.

The Sea of Galilee holds life within itself and nurtures the life around it. It is fed by many small streams and by the waters of the River Jordan and the River Yarmuk. And as the sea is fed, so it feeds—the mother-center of the Galilee family. The lake teems with fish and the shoreline is lush with greenery. From this lake, men extract their food, quench their thirst, and take water to cleanse their bodies. Just as woman in her many roles is known by many names—daughter, wife, or mother—so is the Sea of Galilee known as Lake Kinnereth, or Tiberias, or Gennesaret.

People gathered round the lake for pleasure and sustenance. So to these well-populated shores came Jesus, entering the cities beside the water to cast His nets for the souls of men. And the first to be drawn in were His disciples. They were men of the land and men of the sea, tillers and fishers:

Peter, Andrew, James, and John—Fire, Water, Air, and Sea

Phillip, Judas, Simon, and Bartholomew—Fish, Field, Flower, and Tree

Matthew, Thomas, Thaddeus, and James—Mountain, Plain, River, and Valley

He gathered them together and taught them to reap a new harvest, to bring to shore another kind of catch. Day by day the Word took root, and day by day the believers grew in number. Mother Galilee gave of her children, and to these children Jesus gave of His Father.

Some teachers have few pupils, others have many. Jesus attracted uncountable numbers to His side. And a day came when there was not space enough for Himself and the multitudes who pressed round Him. Jesus turned to the Sea of Galilee and the Sea became His dais. As the crowds stood listening on the shore, He spoke from a boat anchored in the middle of the lake. And as the rippling water soaked into the sand beneath their feet, so His Lessons were absorbed by His land-bound listeners.

Since the land was fertile all manner of things grew there, among them Jesus and the fruits of the Kingdom. The land today is a reflection of that past, for the past was born of the land, raised upon the land, and locked between the layers of earth and the passage of time.

The sea that is seen today is the sea they saw. And as a plant that grows on the shores of the Kinnereth, Jesus matured beside the lake.

Jesus traveled from city to city in the Galilee but the place
to which He went most often was Capernaum.

A stone-built seaside city, Capernaum was prosperous and
supported a large synagogue in which He often spoke. The
disciples Simon and Andrew were men of Capernaum and
their home was His home.

From Capernaum He often journeyed to Chorazin and
Bethsaida, and the People of these cities knew Him well.

In all these places Jesus harvested affliction like a farmer
reaps corn, but while what is left in the wake of the farmer is an
empty field, that which remained behind Jesus was the seed
of wonder and the stalk of health.

For He was besieged by the unfortunate and He took upon
Himself the mantle of their misery. Many sought Him and
many were cured. And the doctrine of repentance was carried
around the land on the wings of His wondrous deeds.

A king offered his palace to a beggar. But the beggar wanted some sign that the king was a king and the palace was a palace. The king showed the beggar many fine things from his palace, but the beggar was not yet satisfied. His disbelief wounded the king and the king offered the palace no longer.

Let the king be likened unto Jesus and the palace unto the Kingdom of God which He foretold. Let Capernaum, Chorazin, and Bethsaida be likened unto the beggar in his disbelief, and therein lies the reason these cities flourish no more.

Capernaum and Chorazin are silent, empty ruins, and there remains not a trace of Bethsaida. Beneath the weight of His pronouncements against them, these cities crumbled. For Jesus offered them the Kingdom and they asked for signs of the Messenger.

Oh, unbelieving cities! If your lonely stones were warmed by human life once again, would you know Him any better than before?

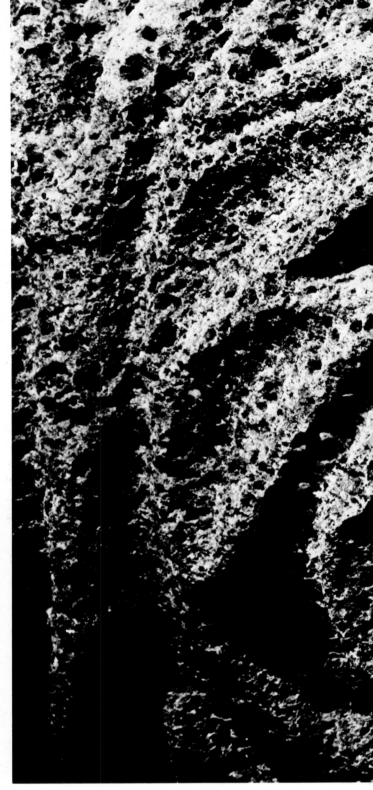

Time, not man, is the true conqueror of the land. In
Chorazin and Bethsaida, men carved stones, erected
monuments, and built great cities surrounded by great walls.
They labored as if their works would endure forever. But Time
has decreed that men perish; their cities crumble. A pillar, a
basin, a carefully arranged circle of rocks that was perhaps the
foundation of some important public building, are testimony to
a once flourishing community. Many cities have died this way,
ravaged by the hand of time after the men disappear. Time
mocks the men who have left behind them memorials to their
culture. Weeds grow, columns become dust, winds eat away
the finely sculpted stone. But Time is not altogether brutal,
for the destruction is slow, and many generations are allowed
to recollect the past through the relics that linger upon the land.

Magdala is now a ruined village. Half a wall, a house without a roof—that is all that remains of this ancient, busy shore town. In Magdala was born Mary Magdalene, who followed Jesus unto the hour of His death and further. The Apostle John has written that she knelt at the foot of the cross and she watched and waited beside His tomb. It was Mary of Magdala who was the first to discover that Jesus had risen from His bier.

Mons
Olivarum

Gethsemani
Bethania
Bethphage
Cedron

JERUSALEM
Golgotha sive Calvariae Mons

ITURAEA

Jordani fl.

Ennon

Bethania

Desertum

Ephrem

Jericho

Sodoma

Gomorra

ichar

MARIA

Cedron

JERUSALEM

Bethania

Desertum

Bethlem

Emmaus

Rama

JUDAEA

Arimathaea

Montes

UM

Studia 200

Italica

AEGYPTUS

A R A B I A E . P A R S

UP TO JERUSALEM

"...he took the twelve disciples aside, and said to them, 'Behold, we are going up to Jerusalem; and the Son of man will be...mocked and scourged and crucified...'"
(Matthew 20:17–19)

In the environs of Jerusalem, with its great shrines commemorating so many important events of Our Lord's life and death, are other significant sites: Ein Kerem, Bethany, Bethphage, and Emmaus. And to the east of the city there is a road—the road to Jericho. This highway and this town both played an important part in His ministry.

Ein Kerem Today the village of John the Baptist is a suburb of the new Jerusalem, close to its busy streets with their shops, traffic, and towering blocks of flats. The village remains a haven of peace and serenity even while, on the hilltops to the east, the tall buildings of the new city stand for all the world like an advancing army halted in its tracks by a sudden vision of peace and reconciliation.

Ein Kerem was always a place of quiet beauty, the scene of joy and promise. Today it has become a refuge for artists and musicians who are striving to protect and preserve the tranquil atmosphere of the ancient village, the birthplace of the forerunner of Christ.

However, it is not certain where John was born. The New Testament (Luke 1:39) refers only to "a city of Judah" in the hill country, but tradition identifies the "city" with Ein Kerem. The mention of Ein Kerem has long evoked reference, direct or indirect, to John the Baptist. In our own time guides remain faithful to this ancient tradition and refer to the town as "Saint John's in the Mountains."

Mary's aged cousin Elizabeth and her old husband the priest Zachary lived here. Zachary, doubting God's word that his wife would bear a son, had been stricken dumb until all that had been foretold would come to pass. Their home was in the town proper, but, like most families with any means, they would have had a small piece of land outside the town for the growing of fruit and vegetables. Perhaps there was a small house there, where they could escape the summer heat and smells of the crowded village. It was there, to the hilltop on which today stands the exquisite Chapel of the Visitation, that the visiting Mary came on that day long ago soon after the angel had brought her her own wonderful news. And when Elizabeth saw her, she was inspired to say joyfully: "Blessed are you among women, and blessed is the fruit of your womb." Then she added, "And why is this granted me, that the mother of my Lord should come to me? For behold, when the voice of your greeting came to my ears, the babe in my womb leaped for joy" (Luke 1:42-44). And Mary answered in the great and wonderful canticle of the Magnificat: "My soul doth magnify the Lord and my spirit doth rejoice in God my Saviour...," these words spoken, according to the tradition, in the grotto that now lies below the Church of the Visitation. This church, designed by Antonio Barluzzi and completed only in 1955, replaced older ruined structures. The Crusaders erected churches over an ancient well and a nearby rock in which, according to legend, Elizabeth hid the infant John from Herod's slaughter of the children.

At the foot of the hill is the spring which gives its name to Ein Kerem, the "Spring of the Vineyard" or, in another version, the "Bounteous Spring." All manner of legends attach to the spring: that Mary drank of its waters during her visit with Elizabeth; and that Elizabeth washed John's small clothes there, for which reason Christians still use the spring's water for washing on the eve of the Feast of Saint John.

The present Church of Saint John is a modern structure, the latest of a series of churches built, destroyed, and built again on the traditional site of the birthplace of John in the home of Zachary and Elizabeth. The main altar within the upper church is dedicated to Saint John, while in the grotto, within a hollow niche under the marble altar, is a plaque with a sunburst of rays and the simple Latin sentence, "Here the Precursor of the Lord was born."

It was here, also, on the eighth day after his birth, that the friends and relatives of the family came to celebrate John's circumcision. They wanted to name the child after his father, but Elizabeth refused, saying that his name must be John. They appealed to the father, and he wrote on the table, "His name is John." Then Zachary's mouth was opened and he spoke for the first time since he had been struck dumb at the moment the angel had told him that Elizabeth was to bear a child. And he uttered the wonderful words of the Benedictus, "Blessed be the Lord God of Israel, for he has visited and redeemed his people..."

One of the ancient shrines discovered below the present church contained an ornate mosaic with the Greek inscription "Hail, Martyrs of God," reminding us that John was to end his days as a martyr at the hands of Herod.

Near Ein Kerem are other memorials to innocent martyrs. On one hill overlooking the town stands Yad Vashem, monument to the memory of the six million Jews so ruthlessly martyred in our own day. Not far away is the John F. Kennedy peace forest and memorial. Ein Kerem is a place of peace in which to remember great tragedies and not despair. For did not the Child who was born here grow up to proclaim, "the Kingdom of Heaven is at hand," and did not that Babe, Whose mother came here on a visit to her cousin, promise us eternal victory over death and evil?

Bethany Where the road to Jericho runs down

from Jerusalem, there stands the little village of Bethany. It is still a quiet hamlet, in which it is easy to imagine the village as it was when Our Lord would come here to recuperate in the home of His loving friends, Mary, Martha, and Lazarus, before setting out once more on His arduous task.

We all know the story of how, during one of those visits, Martha was so occupied with household cares she had no time to talk with her guest. When she upbraided her sister for not helping her, Our Lord rebuked her with the gentle words, "Martha, Martha, you are anxious and troubled about many things. One thing is needful!"

It was in Bethany, too, that Our Lord ate at the house of Simon the Leper and a woman poured precious ointment over His head (Matthew 26:6-13), arousing the complaint that the ointment could have been sold and the money given to the poor. "The poor," Jesus answered, "you have always with you, but you will not always have me."

Of course, the great event that took place in Bethany was the raising of Lazarus from the dead, after he had been in his tomb four days (John 11). We can follow Martha as she goes out to meet Jesus on the road leading into the town and utters the sorrowful words, "Lord, if you had been here, my brother would not have died." Yet when Our Saviour tells her "I am the resurrection and the life," she makes that wonderful profession of faith: "Yes, Lord; I believe that you are the Christ, the Son of God." In the Scriptures only one other person makes this declaration and that is Peter, just before Our Lord gave unto him the keys of the Kingdom of Heaven (Matthew 16:15-19). Nor does Martha go unrewarded. She calls Mary, and the two sisters bring Him to the tomb. Jesus calls, "'Lazarus, come forth.' And the dead man comes out from the tomb, his hands and feet bound with bandages and his face wrapped with a cloth."

Today we can visit the tomb thought to be that of Lazarus and be fairly certain it is the real one. Such an event was surely a topic of supreme interest to the inhabitants of Bethany, and the tomb must always have been pointed out to visitors. Origen (second century) speaks of it. In the sixteenth century the present mosque was built over the tomb and the original entrance sealed. In 1612 the Father Custos of the Holy Land, on payment of a large sum, obtained permission to have the present stairway cut out. Thus pilgrims were once more able to visit the venerable shrine.

The present Franciscan church built in 1953 is the fourth on the site. The first one was erected in the fourth century and destroyed either by fire or earthquake in the fifth century. A new church was built, only to be destroyed in its turn and replaced by the Crusaders in the twelfth century. Queen Melisande built a large Benedictine nunnery here, too, the remains of which can still be seen today. It was here that Pope Paul made his first stop at a shrine during his historic pilgrimage to the Holy Land in 1964.

The Arab name for Bethany today recalls the miracle: The town is called el Azariyeh, which comes from the name Lazarus. The Hebrew words azar yeh mean "God helped."

Bethphage This village (its name means House of Green Figs) was on the Mount of Olives, about half a mile above Bethany. All that is to be seen here today is the Franciscan church and several houses. Nonetheless this is the traditional site at which Jesus met Martha and then her sister Mary as He was on His way to Bethany after the death of Lazarus. And it was from Bethphage that He began the first Palm Sunday triumphal procession into Jerusalem. Both these events are marked by a single stone known as the Stele of Bethphage which is in the Franciscan church. For at some early time devout pilgrims hollowed out the sacred stone upon which, tradition says, Jesus stood when He met Martha and Mary, and from which He mounted the foal to begin His journey on that first Palm Sunday. The tradition is definite that there was a stone here, but the one to be seen in the church at present is far too tall to have been used as a mounting block. Nonetheless, in the 12th century it was decorated with fine paintings of the most delicate workmanship, comparable to the illuminations of a missal rather than an ordinary fresco. A good portion of the painting has vanished, but enough remains to indicate the incidents originally portrayed. Depicted on one side of the stone are the ass and her foal; on another, the people bearing palms; and on the third, Mary and Martha at the feet of Jesus with the resurrection of Lazarus in the background. Today it is from this church that the Palm Sunday procession begins. Surely this procession, here in Jerusalem, is the most significant one anywhere on earth. Thousands of people from every corner of the globe assemble to honor their Lord and Saviour by following in His footsteps. Bearing long palm branches in their hands and singing their native hymns, the throngs of people move slowly up the east slope of the Mount of Olives, over its crest, and down the far side. Reaching the valley of Kidron the procession continues up the hill to the city walls, then in through St. Stephen's gate to the Church of St. Anne. Here the ceremony ends with the blessing of the multitude. It has long been the custom for the throngs to wave their palm branches during the blessing, and the sound of the rustling of the thousands of palm branches is something never to be forgotten.

But only five days after that first Palm Sunday Jerusalem was to witness another great crowd clamoring for Jesus' death. Only one short week separated His triumph from His supreme test, His victory over death and His Glorious Resurrection.

Emmaus This is a village on the western side of Jerusalem. On the first Easter Sunday Cleopas and his son Simeon were returning from Jerusalem full of wonder at the events of the past few days. There had been the terrible occurrences of Friday, when all they had believed in seemed utterly destroyed. They must have mourned all through the Sabbath until on Sunday morning the astonishing rumors began to spread. Some of the women had said the tomb was empty, and the almost unbelievable news of the resurrection was noised abroad. And as Cleopas and Simeon walked down the road from Jerusalem they talked of those momentous events. Then a stranger suddenly appeared, and walking with them marvelously explained the prophecies of the Old Testament and connected them with the events of the past few days. Arriving home, father and son urged the stranger to remain with them and share their humble evening meal. He took the bread and blessed it, and as He vanished from their sight, their eyes were opened. Gone was all weariness. Cleopas and Simeon arose in haste and hurried back to Jerusalem to spread the wondrous news.

In Emmaus we can still see a bit of the actual Roman street that came from Jerusalem, and we walk on those ancient stones with a feeling of sharing that incident told of in the Gospel. On either side of the street are the remains of houses rebuilt by the Crusaders but once more fallen into ruin. Over the remains of the traditional house of Cleopas is the Church of St. Cleopas.

Jericho The road to Jericho runs down from Jerusalem through a barren landscape of rocky gorges and bare, blistered hills, piled one against the other, with no relief of shade, verdure, or shelter. This is a land of loneliness and desolation, the surrounding hills providing an ideal hiding place for the robber bands that, over the centuries, lurked in waiting for pilgrims and travelers, their age-long prey.

This is the way Our Lord and His disciples took between Jerusalem and Galilee. As was said before, to avoid crossing the territory of the Samaritans, it was usual for Jews to descend to Jericho, cross the Jordan nearby, and go north through Perea on the east bank of the river, crossing back at the Sea of Galilee. It made a long, weary, and dangerous journey. The many sanguinary names which attach to this road—the Chastel Rouge of the Crusaders, for example, and the Khan el Ahmar (Ascent of Blood), which is one of the possible sites of the Inn of the Good Samaritan—may be explained by the red coloring of some of the rocks at certain times of the day. But the many bloody deeds these rocks have witnessed make the names doubly appropriate.

The account Our Lord gave of the man going down to Jericho who fell among thieves and was robbed, stripped, and left lying half-dead by the roadside (Luke 10:30-36) would have seemed in no way far-fetched to His listeners. Nor, sadly enough, would they have found it hard to believe that the priest and the Levite who came along would "pass by on the other side," fearing a trap or the inconvenience of getting involved. And have we ourselves yet learned to put into action, without exception, our words of charity and mutual help? Jesus pointed the moral by noting that the next traveler to pass down the road was a Samaritan—one of that people utterly despised and shunned by the Jews. Yet it was the Samaritan who "had compassion on him and went to him and bound up his wounds...set him on his own beast and brought him to an inn, and took care of him." From this action there evolved the term "good Samaritan," a synonym for spontaneous kindness and charity. At about the half-way point between Jerusalem and Jericho, there are the ruins of a Turkish Khan (or inn) known as Khan Hathrour. Traditionally this is known as the site of the Inn of the Good Samaritan, and the choice seems reasonable. There was some water to be found here and, surely, a traveler would be refreshed by a rest stop during his tedious journey. Our Lord must often have passed this way with His disciples; He must have known the inn of which He spoke, and His eyes must have roamed over these desolate hills.

As the road descends and approaches Jericho the landscape becomes even bleaker. Surely there never was life here, nor could there ever be any. Then, suddenly before us, we see the brilliant green of the palm groves and fruit orchards of Jericho.

When Jesus came to Jericho, on His last journey to Jerusalem, a blind beggar was sitting by the wayside. Hearing a great throng passing, the beggar inquired what this meant and, when told, he cried out to Jesus for help. Those who were with Our Lord tried to quiet him, but he persisted until Jesus heard him, had him brought forward, and restored the beggar's sight (Luke 18:35-43).

There follows the touching story of Zacchaeus, chief tax collector. He was rich, and doubtless he was hated and despised by his fellow Jews. But to make sure he would not miss his chance to see Jesus, he ran on ahead and climbed up a tree, "for he was small of stature." Just imagine his joy when Jesus halted below, called to him, and told him that He would be a guest in his house that very day.

Zacchaeus' words while entertaining Jesus in his home, "Behold, Lord, the half of my goods I give to the poor; and if I have defrauded anyone of anything, I restore it fourfold" (Luke 19:8) show that at heart he was a truly just man. Once again Jesus had chosen one of the most despised of men and revealed his humanity. Surely these two incidents are, like Jericho itself, a beautiful oasis of hope in a desert of despair.

There are really three Jerichos. The first, the oldest fortified city on the face of the earth, is today a great mound of stones and scattered shards of pottery, with a stone tower dating back close to Adamic times. This was the city Joshua destroyed and which, because of a divine prohibition, was never rebuilt. In the ninth century Ahab built another city close by (I Kings 16:34), and it was this Jericho, embellished and expanded by Herod, which was the city Jesus knew. Today the site of this city, too, is no more than a heap of ruins. Herod's wondrous palace of Cypros, with its beautiful gardens, has long since crumbled to dust, their beauty and luxury as dead as the cruel tyrant who called them into being and who drew his last breath within their shelter.

The secret of the richness of Jericho's soil is the city's year-round warm climate—it lies, like the Dead Sea close by, 250 meters below sea level—and its abundant supply of water. No wonder when the ancient Hebrews sighted Jericho after their years of wandering in the desert they called the Promised Land a land of milk and honey!

Modern Jericho stands on the site of the city the Crusaders built at the very foot of the ancient hill. From the top of this hill one has a panoramic view of the city with its date palms, orange orchards, banana groves, fig trees, and vineyards. It is easy to understand why Herod loved his "City of Palms" and to judge how gladly the travelers of his time must have welcomed its greenness.

Turning our backs on the modern city, we look to the towering cliffs behind it and see, half-way up, the Greek Orthodox Monastery of the Quarantine—the traditional area of Our Lord's Forty Days of fast in the wilderness. At the very top of the mountain is a walled enclosure, the site of the third and last temptation (Matthew 4:8). The view from the mountain top is stupendous. It is easy to visualize the devil showing Our Lord first the luxuriance of Jericho, then the kingdoms of the world in all their glory and offering them to Jesus in return for one act of worship. Now those glorious cities and mighty empires are turned to rubble, desolation, and oblivion. So fleeting are the rewards of evil!

Seven kilometers to the east of Jericho is the Jordan River and the traditional site of the Baptism of

Our Lord. Today we, too, can stand beside the stream where John stood when Jesus came to him for baptism. We can remember John's shocked remonstrance: "I need to be baptized by you, and do you come to me?" (Matthew 3:14) and Jesus' answer, "Let it be so now." John consented and "when Jesus was baptized, He went up immediately from the water, and behold, the heavens were opened and He saw the Spirit of God descending like a dove, and alighting on Him; and lo, a voice from heaven saying, 'This is my beloved Son with whom I am well pleased.'" (Matthew 3:16–17).

A short distance to the south lies the Dead Sea, the lowest spot on the face of the earth. Some forty miles long and at its widest about twelve miles wide, the Dead Sea is another lesson in the deceptiveness of the things of this earth. The water is crystal clear and its surface sparkles like the glitter of countless diamonds. Yet so bitter and salty is the water that the taste is intolerable, and even after lying in it for only a short time—in water of this buoyancy one stays afloat without any effort—it has to be washed off with fresh water before it burns the skin.

Across the sea to the east are the mountains of Moab, among them Mount Nebo, on whose summit Moses stood to view the Promised Land. God had decreed that he should not be allowed to cross over the Jordan, and there, among those bleak, forbidding peaks, the lawgiver of Israel died and was buried, and no man knows his grave. There is a charming Arabic folk tale that when the time came for Moses to die, he passed two angels digging in the ground and asked them what they dug. "We are digging a grave for a man," they told him, "but we do not know how long to make it, for we do not know the height of a man." "I am a man," answered Moses, and he lay down in the grave, never to rise again.

Moab was the homeland of Ruth, the Moabitess, whose touching devotion to her mother-in-law Naomi was rewarded by a happy second marriage. Ruth was the grandmother of Jesse and great-grandmother of King David, and thus an ancestress of Jesus.

Moab seems an uninviting area now, yet it played a significant role in the history of Judea. In this land of perpetual summer there were settlements wherever there existed water and a line of fortresses against the desert marauders who posed a perennial threat to Jerusalem and Judea.

A little to the south, along the western shore of the Dead Sea, are the remains of Qumran, the desert home of the Essenes, the religious ascetics who, at the time of Christ, were living in retreat from "the world" and striving for spiritual perfection in this remote spot. They spent their time studying the Scriptures, copying them for others to study, and formulating their doctrines. During the great rebellion against Rome when Jerusalem was destroyed, the Essenes fled from the approaching armies, first carefully hiding their precious manuscripts in inaccessible caves. There they lay for nearly nineteen centuries until an Arab goatboy, climbing to the rescue of one of his flock, chanced upon their hiding place. Thus the famous "Dead Sea Scrolls" were revealed for scholars, and all mankind, to treasure. Here, then, in this seemingly barren desert, on either side of the lower Jordan River, we find such riches: We are reminded of Moses, of Joshua, of Ruth; we commemorate the Baptism of Jesus and His subsequent solitary fasting in preparation for His mission. We recall His mercy to the poor and afflicted and His kindness to those whom the world despised.

We tend to think of Christ's teachings against the background of the green hills of Galilee and its beautiful lake, but there are great lessons to be learned here, too, in the burning, barren desert.

Jerusalem was founded upon the stark, unyielding rock of the Judean Highlands, and from this city roads radiated like arteries from the heart. In the time of Jesus there were three routes that led the traveler to Jerusalem. The eastern trail led through the Jordan Valley. The western route followed the coastal plain. The middle road scaled the Samarian Highlands. The Samarian route was the shortest and was the way to the Holy City most often chosen by Jesus and His disciples.

If the heart is turned toward God, the feet turn toward Jerusalem. For Jerusalem is a holy siren that sets each soul to crying out.

The road that led to Jerusalem could be long, filled with people bound across the sun-hot rocks to fulfill some spiritual duty, and lined by men hungry for news and a New Word. The journey to Jerusalem could be difficult and slow if the pilgrim needed to stop along the way, just as when a ladle of drink is passed among thirsty people, each must drink from it, thereby slowing its progress. So it was with the Son of Man when He passed by thirsty men who all wanted to sip of His eternal waters.

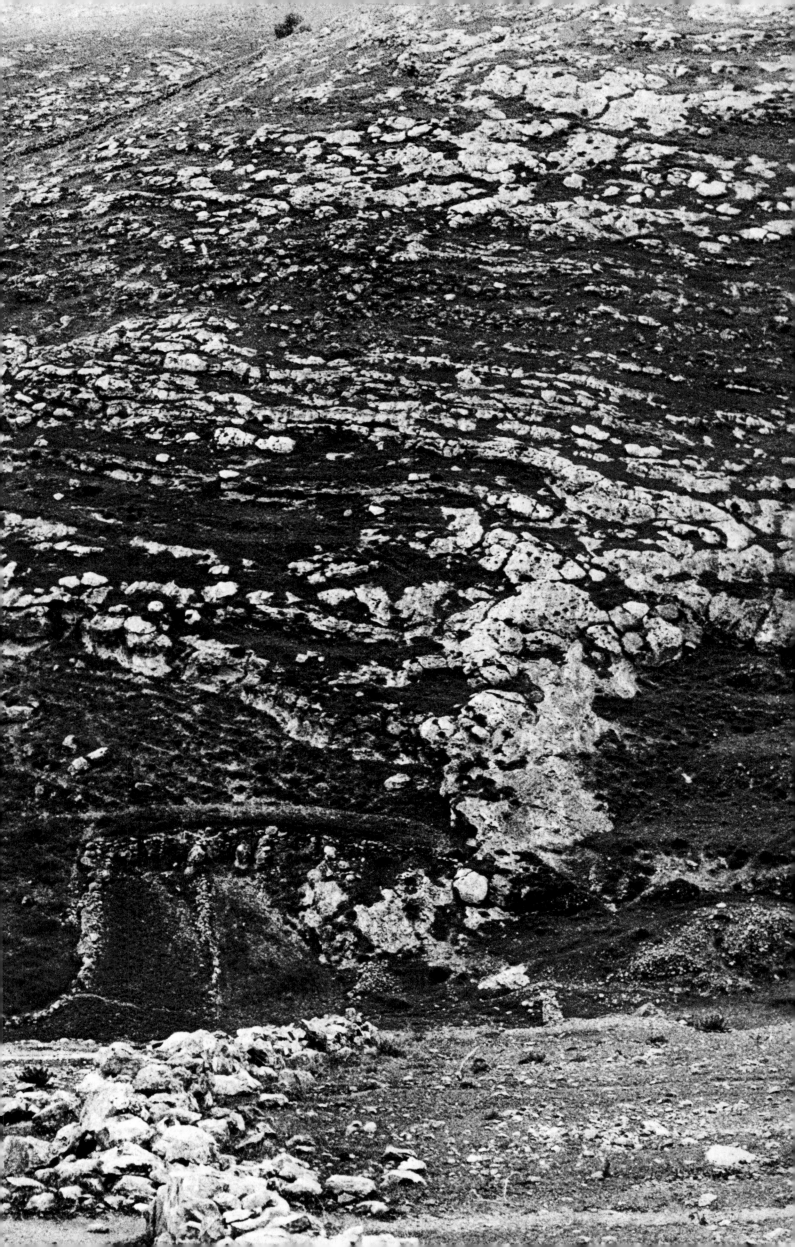

The surface of man's world is made up of his flesh, his struggles, the taint of his blood. And these things penetrate into the entrails of the earth and are spewed back again onto the aching contours of the land which seem to shout, "We are the memorial to all that has happened here; look and remember."

Just as the River Jordan follows a predetermined course, so did John the Baptizer and Jesus Whom he baptized. And after the waters of the Jordan have rushed forward, the riverbed bears the imprint of their passage. John and Jesus, more powerful than the rushing waters, left behind in the riverbed an indelible message. For in this river the precursor baptized the Son, as it had been written that he must.

This middle road to Jerusalem that extended between Galilee and the Judean Highlands passed through the province of Samaria. The people of Samaria were friends to none other than themselves, and the hostilities of men had destroyed the unity of the land. Galilean travelers avoided Samarian roads. But on His way to Jerusalem, Jesus often traveled through Samaria. On one such journey, He stopped at Jacob's Well, a traditional resting place for travelers. There He spoke with a Samaritan woman. She offered Him water from the well and He offered her immortal waters from His heart.

Samaritans worshipped God at Mt. Gerizim; all other Israelites worshipped in Jerusalem. This was the cause for much hatred and bitterness. So when Jesus was asked, "Who is my neighbor?" He answered the questioner with this parable: A traveler was beaten and robbed by a band of thieves who then left the traveler to die beside the road. Many countrymen of the wounded man passed him by and did not stop to help him. Yet a Samaritan saw the wounded man and disregarded the tradition that made them enemies. The Samaritan traveler changed his route and brought the injured stranger to an inn. He bandaged the man's wounds and paid the innkeeper, and this place was thereafter called the Inn of the Good Samaritan.

With this parable, Jesus sought to end hostility among men, for the spirit of his teaching extended far beyond the transient conflicts and rivalries of the times.

Jericho sits quietly in the Jordan Valley, an old venerated city that has known many great men and witnessed many great deeds. Its buildings are made from mud bricks and its hillsides were once filled with date palms and sycamore trees. On their way to Jerusalem, Jesus and His disciples passed by Jericho. A blind man named Bartholomew was sitting beside the road as they passed. Upon learning that it was Jesus whose footsteps he heard, Bartholomew called out to Him, begging Jesus to restore his sight. All the Apostles have written that the blind man's faith in Jesus cured his affliction. Jesus then entered Jericho and stayed in the home of Zaccheus the tax-collector. Jesus blessed the house for its hospitality and blessed Zaccheus who had sinned much in his life. Zaccheus repented and was forgiven, and it is said that from that time hence he changed his ways.

Tradition has located the site of Jesus' struggle in the
wilderness on a high mountain near the Jordan Valley. The
Crusaders named the mountain Mons Quarantana, Mountain
of the Forty Days. It is also known by the name Jebel
Quruntal, Mountain of Temptation.

Hacked into the craggy cliff is the Greek Orthodox
Quarantine Monastery. Seven monks now inhabit this stone-
faced community where once lived 6,000 monks. The
monastery is but a cluster of small buildings and a chapel, all
furnished simply with wooden objects. Hermit cells are carved
into the mountain itself. For one hundred years, the monastery
has overlooked the rock whereon He sat for forty long days
and nights.

Under Roman rule, the people of Israel suffered persecution and oppression, and the rich lived comfortably upon the backs of the poor. The world of men appeared evil, decadent, and foul. Jesus brought the message of a New Kingdom and many men were comforted. But some men were not comforted and they turned away from the world. They withdrew from the cities and lived as ascetics in the Judean Desert. Amidst the gaunt and barren rock of Qumran, they scourged their bodies and purged their souls in the name of all men. They explored the mysteries of the ancient traditions and sought to obey the laws which the age transgressed. These Essenes, as they were called, abandoned the pleasures of the earth to search for God and sought grace in the mortification of the flesh. They did not know there was another Who walked the land Who offered God and grace through His own body, "Even as the Son of Man came not to be ministered unto, but to minister, and to give His life as a ransom for many." Matthew 20:28

And Jesus went from the water to the wilderness, leaving behind His hidden Nazareth years and stepping into the fated footsteps of the Christ.

In the wilderness He was alone with the spirits that do their macabre dance on the pinnacles of mountains and call out on a black night's breeze. There was no food, no human sound, no soft place to rest the body. In the wilderness He was eternally joined to His purpose, for there the voices which dwell within a man and those which swell beyond him speak loudly. He stayed forty days and emerged girded with the truth and strength that were the pillars of His teaching. Although He went next into the Galilee and began His Public Ministry, His baptism and His sojourn in the wilderness were the first stopping places on the way to Jerusalem. All things that came after were but steps in the passage to His final redemptive act.

A hunter tried to capture a wild beast, but the beast was fierce and cunning and would not be caught. When the man grew weary, the wily creature became the hunter and pursued the man. And the wild beast caught the hunter and devoured him.

The wilderness was just such a wild beast as this. The land was savage and no man could master it. Knowing this, Jesus took Himself into the belly of this creature as its captive. He was clawed by the jagged rocks and swallowed by the shadows of the mountains. He was tormented by the scorching sun and bone-chilled by the cold night air. He was pursued by hunger, thirst, and the desolation of the place. But although He was prey to the wilderness, the wilderness did not destroy Him. The days of isolation and agony made clear to Him the meaning of His mission, and the wilderness set Him free to return to mankind.

Ein Kerem lay peacefully in the shadow of Jerusalem, a
hill town old and quiet. Cypress and pine trees grew there,
green in winter as well as in summer. In this place dwelt the
mother of John the Baptist. Pilgrims now travel to Ein Kerem in
the month of June to celebrate the Feast of St. John the
Baptist. They fill the churches and rejoice that in this village
the Forerunner was born.

As a moth is attracted to light without understanding the
reason, Mary mother of Jesus was drawn to Elizabeth mother
of John. All of her life Elizabeth had been barren, as fruitless
as a stone. And Mary was like an unturned stone. And then
unexpectedly, each was blessed with a miraculous seed. Each
woman became more precious than any precious stone,
transmuted with the light of inner life.

When Elizabeth had carried John for six months, Mary
came to Ein Kerem. The churches of Ein Kerem commemorate
their meeting and preserve in still, consecrated rooms the
manuscripts written in celebration of the occasion. Holy
mother did greet Holy mother and unborn did greet unborn.
Mary stayed with Elizabeth for three months, and although
Jesus was but a promise in her womb, this visit was a part of
the design that would be the pattern of His life.

Bethany rested close to Jerusalem, an oasis of quiet. More often warm than cold, more rocky than flat, it was a stronghold of life on the edge of the desert wilderness. Bethany was a hearthside for Jesus, a place where He could eat and rest, cared for by those who loved Him. And He repaid this love by restoring Lazarus to life.

And mounted on a donkey as it had been foretold, it was from Bethany that Jesus began His final journey to Jerusalem.

Ioppa — Shaalbin — Gibeon — Shilo
Iamnia — Modin — Chephrhaams
Rakkon — Harfhemesh — Iabneel — Ithlah — Michmas
Iehud — Bene-berah — Moza — Anath
Mejarkon — Gallim — Kiriath-iearim
Baalah — Ramah — Nob
Gath — Gibethon — Mons Aaron — Giboah Saulis
Gath Rimmon — Ierufalem
Elon — Bethfhemesh — Emaus — Toni Niphtoah
Templum belzebub — Vallis Hinnom
Timnah — Gebah — Zebzah
Dan — Hepher — Zorah — Bethleh
Heg-Amah — Eltekeh — Sepulcrum Sampsonis — Diliam
Adullam — Mispeh — Desertum
Ashdod — Azekah — Shillim
Sorek torens — Beth-marcaboth — Spelunca Dauidis — Iachish
Beth-labaoth — Hareth — Tappuah — Iacktheel
Ziglag — Azm — Be
El-tolad — Baalah — Iim — Migdalga
Balah — Samfana — Hezekah — Zenam
Askalon — Keilah — Nezib — Boukath
Azem — Ain — Bethpalot — Gedor — Kaba
Har.orfufah — Sharuhen — Hebro
Simeon — Danugk — Iarmuth — Sepulcrum Abner
Hazor-fhual — Aenda — Hazar gaddah — Shamir — Humtah
Shebah — Gerar — Anab — Socoh
Efek — Rechoboth — Bethul — Goshon
Maladah
Beersheba — Hormah
Sitnah — Ashtemoth
Bezor tor — Tochen
Gaza — Baalath
DESERTVM — Beer-la-harof
Majuma — Ramah meridionalis — Hezron — Holor
Bered — Hazor — Kerioth
KADESH — Ziph
Rinocoloura — Bealoth — Amam
Fluuius Egipti — Telem — Shema
Hadaltah

Ieticho
Gilgal
Vallis Achor
Debir
Macherus
Adumim
Geliloth
Zeboim
Lasha
Manahath
Vallis Keziz
Lapis Bohan
Ashdoth-Pis
Hazor
Betharabah
Neballat
Enshemesh
Beth-hoglah
hurim
ogel
Kidron flu:
Meddin
ebrah
Nibshan
Socatah
Libnah
Zoar
Spelunca Lot
Spelunca Saulis
Lahmam
Engedi
Kithlish
Defertum
Engedi
Iudah
Iessimon
Ziph
Defertum ziph
ahmam
Hachilah
Sodom
Defertum
Maon
Sela
Maon
Hammahehoth
sepher
Zanoah
Dumah
Carmel
Iezraeal
Iockdeam
Gomorah
rah
Giloh
Iuttah
Eshean
Kedesh
Ithnan
Ianun
Hazor
Adadah
ekah
Beth tappua
Dimonah
Arad
Kinah
ud
Eder
Iagur
Admah

BETHLEHEM

"...In Bethlehem of Judea; for so it is writen by the prophet: 'And you, O Bethlehem, in the land of Judah, are by no means least among the rulers of Judah; for from you shall come a ruler who will govern my people Israel.'" (Matthew 2:5–6)

o the south of Jerusalem lies Bethlehem. Modern pilgrims, who generally no longer approach the town on foot, forfeit much understanding that could be gained from the beauty of the countryside surrounding Bethlehem. Atop a hill a little before the town, the venerable Greek Orthodox monastery of Mar Elias gives the pilgrim his first view of Bethlehem nestling against its hillside. Here is tranquility, a peaceful town whose history has been remarkably undisturbed. Church buildings in Bethlehem have been preserved intact as nowhere else in the Holy Land. Thus a study of the Basilica of the Nativity can link us directly with the many generations of Christians who have worshiped there through the ages.

The place of the Nativity was venerated by the earliest Christians, and it is for that reason that the Emperor Hadrian, in his attempt to paganize Palestine, had the grotto turned into a shrine honoring Adonis. Pagan rites were celebrated in the very place where the Son of God first saw the light of day. When Christianity was liberated under Constantine the Great (A.D. 313), the emperor resolved to adorn three "mystic caves" in the Holy Land that were held specially sacred. One of these was, of course, the grotto of Bethlehem. All signs of pagan worship were removed and work on a magnificent basilica was begun in 326. The plan of the building was remarkably like that of the Anastasis (Church of the Resurrection) in Jerusalem. The central feature, the grotto beneath, was marked from above by an octagonal structure which stood out prominently from the main body of the church. Elegant steps, twenty-six feet wide and two feet high, led up to it from the floor of the church and there was probably an altar in the center of the raised octagon.

The body of the church was almost square in shape, eighty-eight by eighty-six feet. It had a central nave and four aisles, in the manner of classical basilicas. Surviving fragments testify to the rich mosaics that decorated the floor, patterned with geometrical designs as well as motifs of trees, fruits, and domestic birds. Both Saint Jerome, who settled in Bethlehem in 385, and Aethria, who visited the Holy Land as a pilgrim toward the end of the fourth century, have left descriptions of other adornment: rich tapestries, cloth of gold, precious vessels, numerous lamps of various sizes, more mosaics, and rich marbles. From the outset, nothing was thought too costly for the commemoration of Jesus' birth in Bethlehem.

The ultimate fate of Constantine's basilica is still a mystery. Ashes and fragments of charred wood found in the remains suggest that the basilica may have been violently destroyed during the Samaritan rebellion (530-1), but the evidence is not conclusive. Whatever the cause of its destruction, when Christians regained control of the site they set about restoring the shrine on a larger and still more elaborate scale.

It was Emperor Justinian I (527-565) who was responsible for the restoration. His first step in the reconstruction was to level the site, burying the remains of the former basilica under two feet of earth. The dimensions of the original church were enlarged upon by the construction of a narthex, or great porch, at the entrance and at the other end, a transept with an apse on each side, and by an extension of the building eastward to finish in another central apse. Thus a large sanctuary under one roof was fashioned where Constantine's octagon had stood.

The most striking feature of the new building was the magnificent forest of interior columns dividing the church into a nave and four aisles. Symbols of immortality for the ancients, the columns have proven themselves so at Bethlehem, for after fourteen hundred years they still stand intact in their stately ranks. Forty-eight in number, they were hewn from the rose-veined white stone of the surrounding mountains. Their capitals are especially rich, with an abundance of acanthus leaves, each adorned with a small Greek cross in the center. The two middle rows of columns support the upper walls nine meters high on which are placed the beams of the roof. The walls' upper sections are opened by windows placed at intervals corresponding to the spaces between the pillars below.

The major historical wonder of the shrine is that it survived the Persian invasion of 614. That year almost every Christian monument in Palestine was brought down in ruins by the rampaging armies from the north. The reason the Bethlehem basilica was spared is given in a ninth-century Greek document: On arriving at the basilica the Persians "were astonished to see on the façade of the church representations of Persian Magi, who were astrologers, and ancient compatriots of theirs. Out of respect and for love of their forebears they venerated them as if still living and spared the church. It is still standing down to our own time." Thus, a mosaic of the Magi worshiping the child Jesus was responsible for the preservation of one of the great Christian monuments of Palestine.

A second wonder was the survival of Justinian's basilica during the other great period of destruction, that of A.D. 1009 directed from the south by Hakim Fatimid, ruler of Egypt. The Moslems seem to have had an instinctive reverence for the shrine, although legend ascribes the actual sparing of the building to a miracle: "Whilst the unbelievers were striving to destroy the Bethlehem church, the place where Christ was born, all at once a brilliant light appeared and smote them to the ground where they expired forthwith." Thus, the church remained intact.

When the Crusaders came to conquer Bethlehem, a third marvel took place. Although the Moslems adopted a "scorched earth" policy in the countryside around the town and destroyed many Christian monuments, when they finally came out to meet the warriors from the West in 1099 they peacefully surrendered Bethlehem itself, the only event of its kind in Crusader history. The result was that Justinian's basilica was undamaged and once again in Christian hands.

Since the building was so well preserved, the Crusader zeal for architecture could turn only to detail. Decoration was the main object, and in the time of the Latin kingdom the basilica was beautified as never before or since. In our own time the effort would perhaps be scorned as petty vaingloriousness, but this monument, standing through the centuries, could justly portray the story of Christian triumph in the world. So, in addition to remaining a place for prayer, the Bethlehem basilica became a place for instruction through imagery.

Striking mosaics on the inside walls told the story of the Faith from its sources: the Bible and the Church Councils. On the inside wall of the church entrance were shown the Old Testament's most prominent precursors of Christ. Above the columns of the central nave the first frieze showed busts of members of Jesus' family line: on the north side, the genealogy according to Saint Luke; on the south side, that according to Saint Matthew. A higher frieze (south) showed pictures of the first six General Church Councils. Opposite were representations of Provincial or Regional Councils. In the transept and sanctuary, details from the life of Christ and His mother were depicted. Thus attention was gradually drawn to the main feature of the basilica, the Grotto of the Nativity below. The great columns were adorned with images of saints representing all the Crusader nations: Canute and Olaf for Scandinavia, Augustine and Ambrose for Italy, James the Apostle and Vincent for Spain, Leonard for Normandy, Catald (a bishop born in Ireland) for Southern Italy. Following their catholic instinct, the Crusaders wrote all names in both Greek and Latin. The high standard of the mosaic work was continued in painting, sculpture, and stained glass. Little wonder that a Greek visitor, John Phocas (1177), could describe it only in superlatives: perikallestaton naon kai pammegan ("by far the most beautiful and greatest temple").

Although it had survived three earlier invasions, the Bethlehem basilica could not escape the religi-

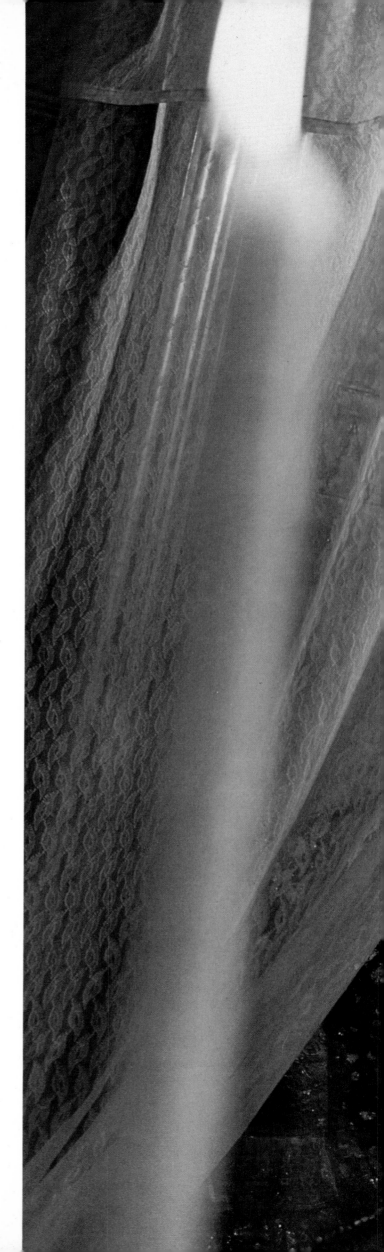

ous, political, and military conflicts that accompanied and followed the Turkish conquest of the Holy Land. Sultan Selim I entered Jerusalem in 1516, and, until General Allenby led the Allied troops into the Holy City on December 9, 1917, Palestine remained a province of the Turkish Empire. A natural result of the Turkish hegemony was that the Greek Orthodox clergy, who formed an integral part of the local population and well understood the Turkish mind, gradually took over the main Christian shrines. Thus from the early seventeenth century the entire upper part of the Bethlehem basilica has been the property of the Greek Orthodox. In the left hand arm of the church the Armenians have two altars. Passing by these altars one enters through a door into the Latin Church of

St. Catherine. Here the Latin Patriarch celebrates the midnight Mass every Christmas eve and after the Mass carries the image of the Infant in solemn procession to the Grotto; there it is kept in the manger until the Feast of Epiphany when it is returned to St. Catherine's Church.

Descending some stairs in St. Catherine's, we arrive at a series of additional grottoes all connected to the main Grotto of the Nativity. These are all actually one grotto but dividing walls were erected to create separate areas. The part nearest the site of Our Lord's birth is called the Chapel of St. Joseph. Here the altar commemorates the angel appearing to Joseph in a dream and telling him to take the Child and His mother and flee into Egypt. In front of the altar, steps lead down to a lower part of the

At the Catholic field have been found the remains of a large Byzantine monastery, near which there is also a grotto such as many shepherds even today use in the winter as a shelter for themselves and their flocks. Beside this grotto the Franciscans have erected a lovely little star-shaped chapel, its dome made of many small circles of light symbolic of the stars in the sky. Below, in the drum of the dome, is a series of angels representing the heavenly choir, and in the center of the chapel stands the simple altar with the adoring shepherds depicted beneath.

The days were not warm and the times were not good. Caesar ruled the world and the world waited. The Augustus issued a decree for a census and the land was heavy with the passage of men and families to their cities of origin. A December wind pushed the travelers across the plains and the hills, past grazing animals whose lives are not changed by the orders of an emperor or the birth of a child. The travelers journeyed across the horizons of bundled watchmen and watchwomen who always hold the silent hope of miracles in their winter-wrapped breasts.

At a pace slower than the pace of many others, Joseph traveled south with Mary, who had the divine promise in her heart. Gradually they made their way from Nazareth into the highlands of Judea to Bethlehem, the city of Joseph's birth. And Bethlehem, opening its gates to admit yet another son returning to be counted, unknowingly welcomed a new Son. For even the will of an emperor is unwittingly bound to the visions of the prophets—and as Micah the Morasthite had declared, from Bethlehem would come a ruler of Israel.

same area, and this area commemorates the Holy Innocents massacred on the orders of Herod in his attempt to cause the death of the Christ Child, the newborn King of the Jews. Passing through a doorway on the right we see the sites of the tombs of St. Jerome, St. Paula, St. Eustochium, and St. Eusebius. When Jerome came to Bethlehem he built a monastery and at the entrance to the sacred grotto he built his own cell, the remains of which we can see today. It was here that he spent so many years writing his great commentaries and making the translation of the Bible which we call the Vulgate.

About a mile southeast of Bethlehem is the area of the shepherds' field. There are actually three fields pointed out today, as no one can say with certainty precisely where in the vicinity the shepherds were.

169

The streets of Bethlehem are nearly always busy. This is a
market town, a well-populated, prosperous place. And yet the
flat-roofed stone houses wedged tightly together, the winding
alleyways—all possess a sense of mystery. For everywhere
signs of the present are intermingled with the shadows of the
past. This is an old city, as old as the Bible, the name of
Bethlehem Ephrathah written in the chapters of Genesis.
Bethlehem belongs now to those who draw the breath of life,
but they must share the city with the memory of those who
breathed here long ago—Ruth and Boaz, Jesse and David,
Joseph, Mary, and Jesus.

172

The man, with the woman and her full womb, chose a grotto on the outskirts of the city because there was no other place to rest. And in that stony cave, Mary bore Jesus. Of that night Luke has written that a mystery appeared in the darkening sky above a shepherds' field and men were visited by angels whose breath was the wind on which floated wondrous tidings. And Matthew has recorded the story of the Magi, Persian priests led by a star and a prophecy to the manger in Bethlehem.

As quickly as news of food spreads among hungry people, so did word of this unique birth fly from mouth to mouth. Stranger spoke to stranger, sharing their curiosity and wonder. And like one who is filled with expectancy and excitement for a gift not yet opened and revealed for what it is, Bethlehem

quivered. For it had been given a gift but did not yet know its nature.

And when time disclosed the gift which Bethlehem had received, the grotto of the birth was enclosed and enshrined with the Church of the Nativity. For such is man's architecture of thanks.

179

The Church of the Nativity is large and cavernous. Its basic structure has stood since before the time of the Crusaders, the first stone having been laid at the decree of Helena, mother of Emperor Constantine, in AD 325. Since that time, many cultures have laid hand to this spot, either to build or to destroy. The Christian community today guards its Church well, and where the Church is aged by time it is being restored.

The vestibule leading to the nave is vaulted and the nave itself is lined by rows of tall columns. The Church is lit by many arched windows and the grotto beneath is illuminated by scores of votive lamps. Marble, mosaics, and silver are testimony to man's generosity and devotion. Tapestries and

*gilt-embroidered cloths hang from ceiling to floor, muffling
voice and footstep.*

*From the choir, a stairway leads down to the Cave of the
Nativity. Long before any church had been built here, the Cave
was reputed to be the birthplace of Jesus and was held sacred by
His following. Now a silver star, inlaid into the stone floor,
marks the place of His birth for all generations to behold. The
Church of the Nativity is custodian and host in that place
where Mother Mary brought forth the baby Jesus "...and laid
Him in a manger; because there was no room for them in the
inn." Luke 2:7*

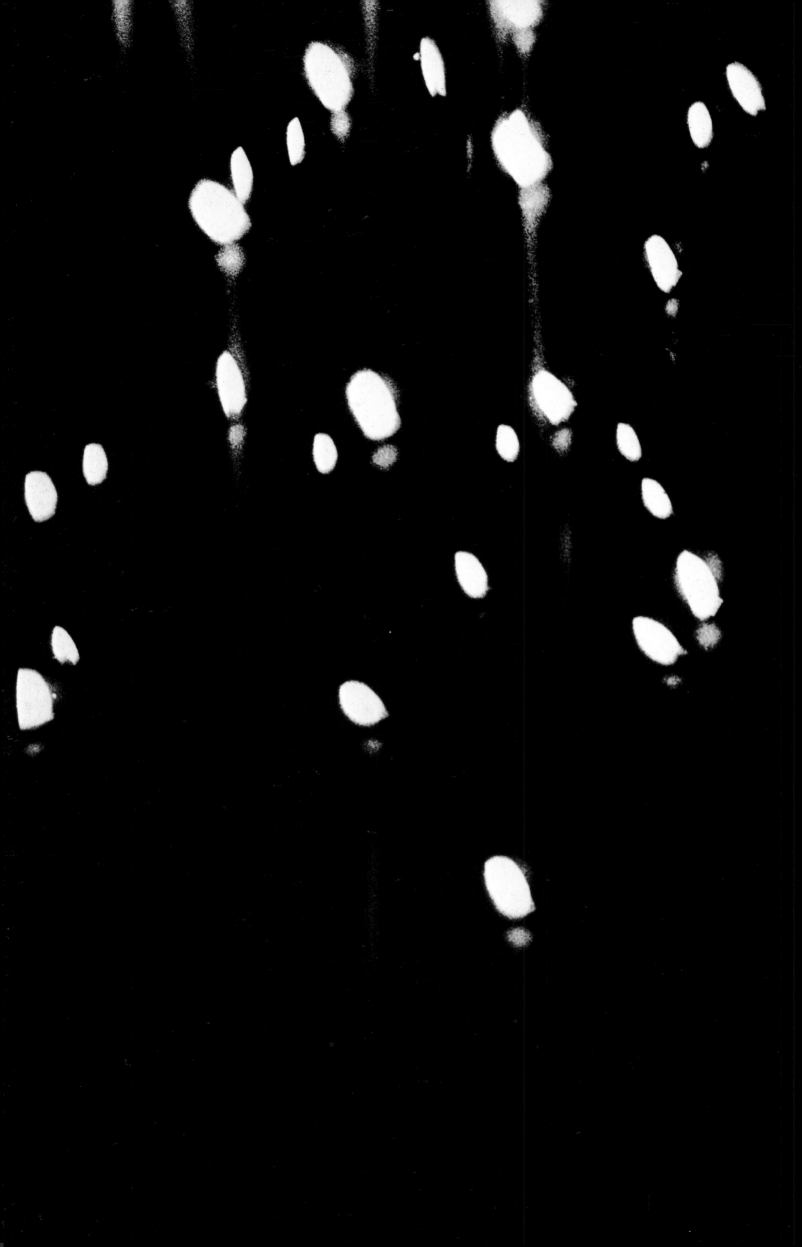

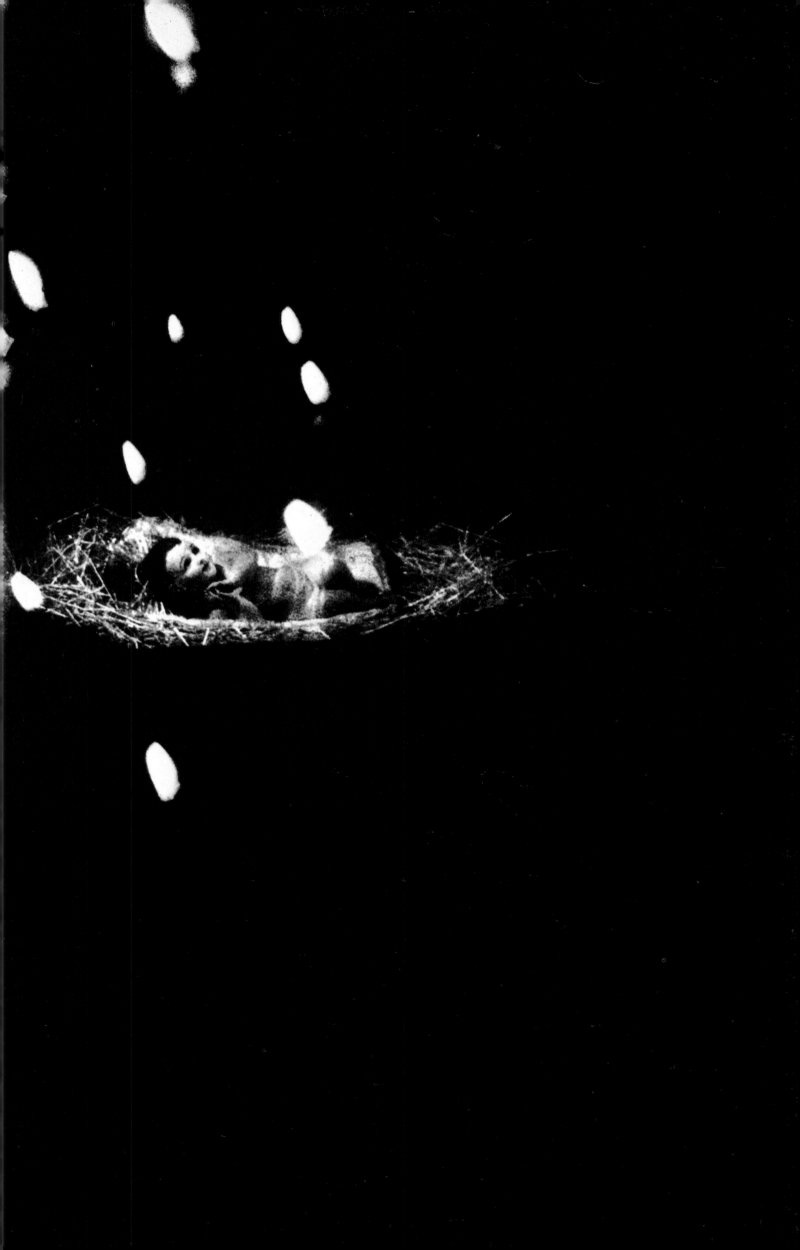

"For unto you is born this day in the city of David, a Saviour which is Christ the Lord." Luke 2:11
"Glory to God in the highest, and on earth peace, good will toward men." Luke 2:14

And so to Bethlehem come Christians of all nations, joined together to remember the birth of their Saviour and the meaning of His coming into the world. On Christmas day the entire city becomes a house of worship and everywhere is heard the sound of voices raised in joyful thanks. Each gust of wind carries with it the scent of incense and candle wax. The Christmas bell in the tower of the Church of the Nativity peals loudly. Carolers line the streets, and along a red-carpeted road the patriarch leads a parade to the Church. In mystery and majesty the scene of the birth is recreated in the Grotto.

On the day that Mary bore Jesus, only some shepherds and three Wise Men traveled to Bethlehem to honor the child and rejoice at His birth. Today, scores of the faithful flock to the city and shoulder to shoulder, voice mingled with voice, they celebrate.

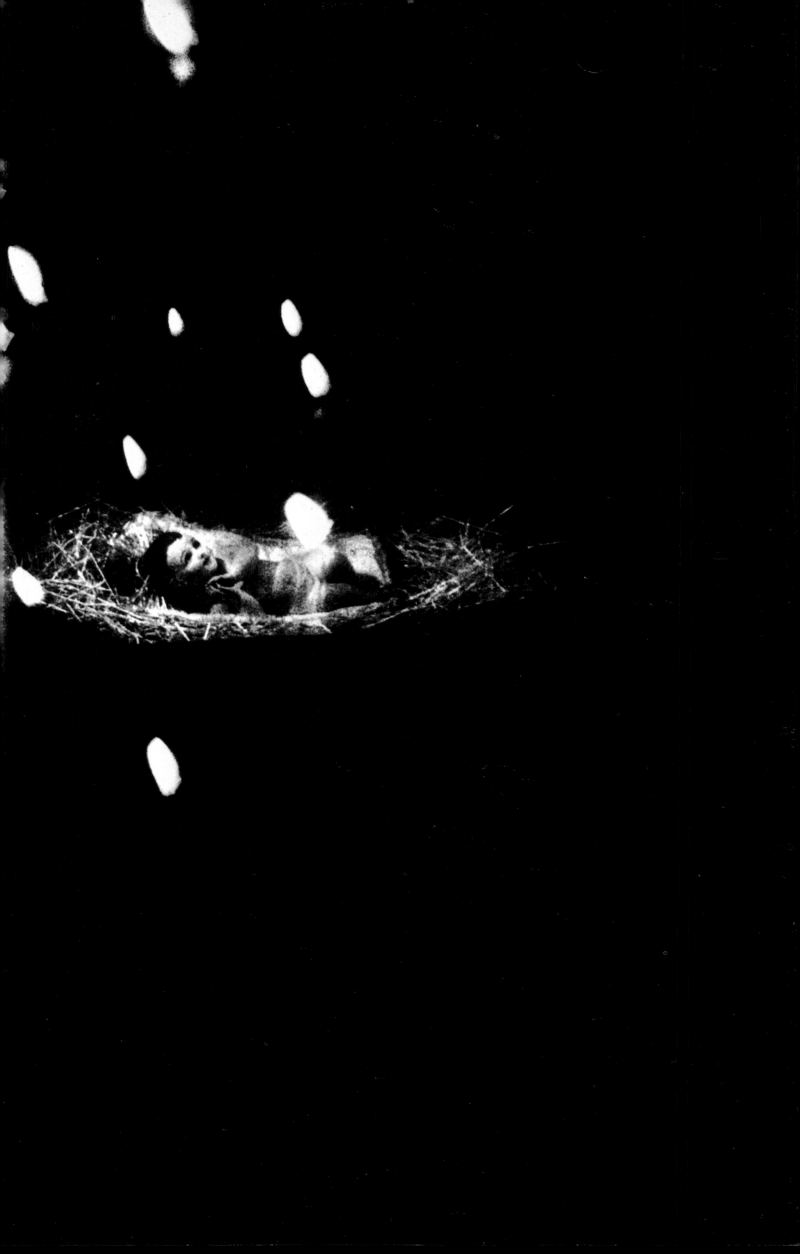

Devotion of the heart is itself a prayer, and no words need be spoken.

All the land is of itself a church, and no walls need surround.

Remembering the angel who appeared to the herdsmen at the hour of Christ's birth, a man may seek out Shepherds' Field. The place becomes a roofless chapel because his faith makes it holy. The litany is recited by the man and by the land and the hour becomes consecrated between them. And in the stillness of this natural chapel, perhaps the praying heart can hear the soft whisper of angels.

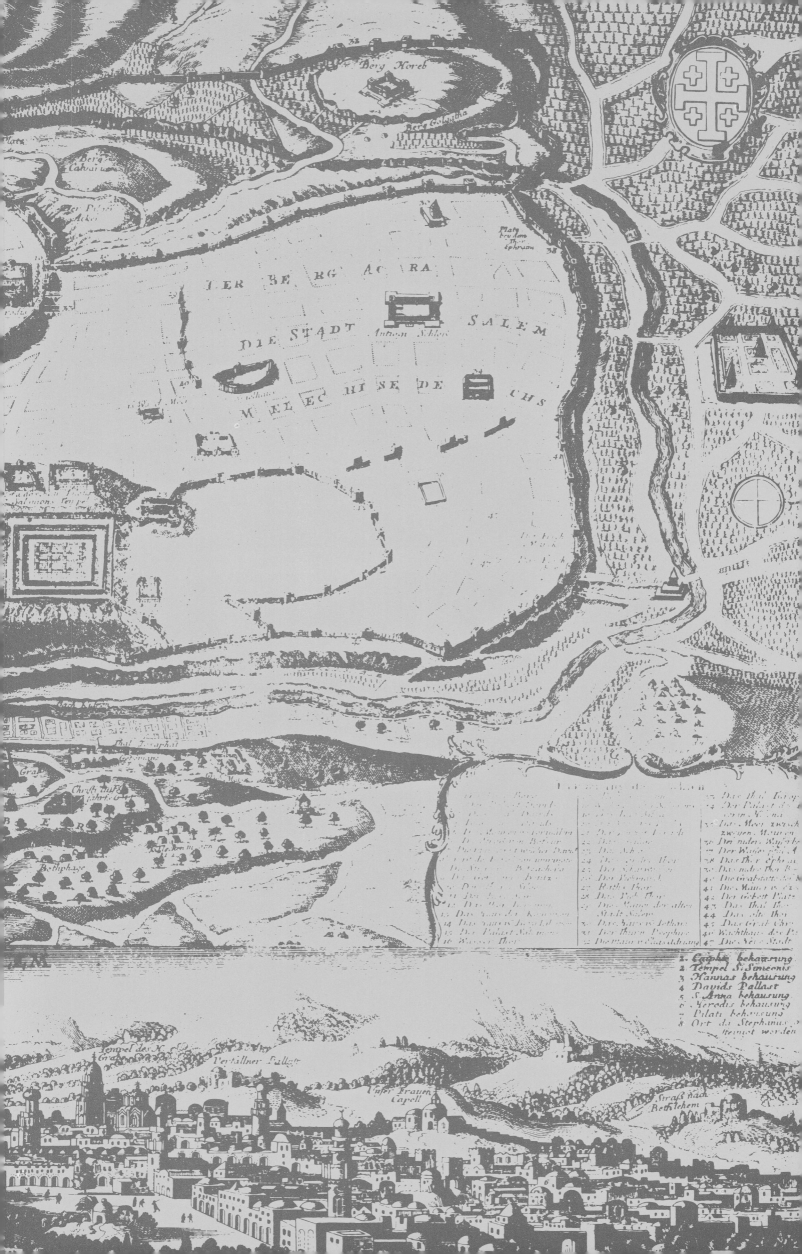

JERUSALEM

"O Jerusalem, Jerusalem, killing the prophets and stoning those who are sent to you! How often would I have gathered your children together as a hen gathers her brood under her wings, and you would not." (Luke 13:34)

How glorious are the thoughts aroused by the name of Jerusalem; how many the memories from the Old and New Testaments: David and Solomon, Isaiah and Jeremiah, our Divine Saviour—His life, death, and resurrection. So often the city has been destroyed, seemingly for all time, only to arise Phoenix-like from its ashes, greater than ever before. So many names have been give to the city: Salem, Aelia Capitolina, Jerusalem, and the Arab name: el Kuds, the Holy.

This city is holy to many peoples of the earth:

For Jews it is the symbol of all their hopes and dreams. Through many centuries they have prayed, "Next year in Jerusalem;" now, for many, a dream realized.

For Christians it is the city of Our Lord. This is the scene of our redemption.

For Moslems it was made holy, not only by the events of the Old and New Testaments, but also as the place from which they believe Mohammed ascended into heaven.

Finally it has become synonymous with our eternal reward, for do we not speak of a heavenly Jerusalem?

Today the stones and bricks of Jerusalem are a living reminder of its glorious past, every street and byway recalling some wondrous deed, every twist and turn of its lanes opening up to our eyes another scene out of the past. But now the city is spreading out across the bare hills. Acres of housing estates blur the landscape earlier generations knew. Only the Old City remains almost unaltered within its walls, the tiny shops and houses lining routes that perhaps Jesus knew and walked.

Following the Six-Day War the whole city is once more a complete entity. This union is more than physical. How well I remember a recent Good Friday when I was leading the English-speaking pilgrims on the Way of the Cross, the way Jesus took to Calvary. We were part of a vast throng from every corner of the globe. Immediately in front of our group was a Baptist contingent from the United States. They were reading from the Scriptures and singing their hymns, and in the pauses between our own prayers, many of my group joined in singing with the Baptists. Behind us was an Anglican or Episcopalian group, also reciting prayers and singing hymns. And so it should be; all Christians following the same Jesus in His spirit of love.

Through the centuries, despite all risks, men have striven to reach this holy city. In the past when pilgrims set out for the Holy Land, they took sorrowful leave of their loved ones, well knowing how slight was the chance that they would ever meet again on this earth. They faced the perils of strange and dangerous lands, of stormy seas and lurking brigands. Yet they set out gladly on their perilous journey for love of their Lord Who had suffered and died in this blessed city. Today travel is swift and safe and pilgrims come in vast numbers to see and know the city of Jerusalem.

The finest and most unforgettable view of the holy city is from the summit of the Mount of Olives, and the best time to see it is in the early morning. At that time the ancient walls and the panorama of domes, spires, and minarets are bathed in a golden hue, seeming to hover in a dreamlike unreality. The very air of Jerusalem is filled with the sounds of prayer—the sonorous music of a hundred church bells; the shrill cry of the muezzins, rising to heaven like a cloud of incense, calling the faithful to prayer. The incense that once rose from the Temple of Jerusalem has long been snuffed out, but the prayers still rise, to remind us all that this is the Holy City. And it is a real city. Beyond the Old City that slopes down toward us from the west lies a whole complex of modern buildings with streets and shops, hotels, museums, government offices, and a university. But what has brought us to this spot are the holy places.

From our vantage point on the Mount of Olives we can see, on our left, the great church of the Dormition Abbey with its accompanying tower. Built by Kaiser Wilhelm II, this church marks the traditional site of Mary's last days on earth and the place where she fell into her final sleep (dormitio: Latin for falling asleep). In the foreground lies the vast expanse of the Temple area, the Haram-as-Sharif, with the two great mosques, the Aksa and the Dome of the Rock. In the center of the city we can see clearly the double domes of the Church of the Holy Sepulchre; next to them, the white tower of the German Lutheran Church of the Redeemer. Towering over the roofs of the city is the spire of the Church of St. Saviour, the Catholic parish church of Jerusalem. On the horizon to the right we can see the small mosque that marks the tomb of the prophet Samuel. The height upon which it stands is known as the Hill of Joy, for from this place pilgrims in the Crusader period had their first view of the city.

Behind us to the east, close to where we stand, lies the traditional spot from which Our Lord ascended into heaven. Also to the east is the Church of the Pater on the site of Constantine's great basilica, the Eleona, marking the place where the Apostles were first taught the prayer of prayers, "Our Father."

As we are descending the Mount of Olives, we traverse the traditional way by which Our Saviour made His triumphal entry into Jerusalem on that first Palm Sunday. Halfway down stands the Chapel of Dominus Flevit ("the Lord wept"), where He paused on that day and, foreseeing the destruction of Temple and city, wept over them. At the foot of the hill He would have passed close to the spot in the olive garden where in but four days' time He would sweat blood in an agony beyond man's understanding. Today, a great basilica stands on the site, a church filled with deep shadows, symbolic of the terrible shadow that darkened the very soul of Christ on that first Holy Thursday. Nearby is the grotto where one of His own chosen was to betray Him.

We then pass the tomb of the Blessed Virgin Mary and ascend the steep hill to St. Stephen's Gate, also known as the Lions' Gate, through which we take our first step into the unfamiliar world of the Old City.

We find ourselves almost at once in front of St. Anne's. Entering by a small inconspicuous door, pilgrims are usually very surprised at finding themselves in a great open-air space, partially a garden and partially an excavated site. We pass beneath the delicate lacy branches of wild pepper trees and see before us a lovely Crusader church, in fact the finest Crusader structure extant in the Holy Land. Here, tradition tells us, Joachim and Anna, Mary's parents, were living when she was born. A member of the Priestly family, Joachim at the time was serving his term as a priest in the Temple, and for this reason had come to Jerusalem from his home in far-off Sepphoris. The site of St. Anne's is also holy as the location of the Pool of Bethesda, that vast double pool with its surrounding porticoes, where Our Lord cured the paralytic who had lain there some thirty-eight years. Part of the great pool lies before us, carefully unearthed by the archeologists. We can also see remnants of the Byzantine church destroyed in the seventh century. Indeed in this small area have been found remains from the fifth and twelfth centuries, as well as from the time of Christ. It is a fitting preparation for what to expect in Jerusalem.

Returning to the street we proceed up a slight hill, upon which stood the fortress-palace built by Herod the Great and named by him the "Antonia" in honor of his friend and patron, Mark Anthony. Part of the area of this structure is now covered by the Franciscan Biblical School of the Flagellation. Across from the entrance of the Franciscan property is a Moslem boys' school. This is the site of the first station of the Way of the Cross. In the Franciscan compound stands a chapel commemorating the scourging of Our Lord, which took place somewhere very close to this spot. Also in the compound

stands the chapel of the second station of the Way of the Cross, where Jesus was given His cross to carry to Calvary.

Leaving the Flagellation we continue a short distance along the street to the Convent of the Sisters of Sion, which also stands on the site of Herod's Antonia. Before entering we notice a large arch spanning the street, with part of its spring disappearing into the wall of the convent. Entering the building we proceed to the Church of Ecce Homo, in which the great arch coming from the street continues on to form a smaller arch which frames the simple altar.

This arch, the Church of Ecce Homo, and the Antonia have a special significance. The Antonia was the headquarters of the praetorium, and thus a Gentile place. No good Jew, therefore, would enter it, as he would thereby become unclean and would have to undergo several days of special ritual before he was "clean" again and able to take part in the prayers and ceremonies in the Temple. Accordingly, on the day that was to be recognized as the first Good Friday, surely Jews would not enter the Antonia, for the Great Pesah began at sunset that very day. But Pilate, who had come from his capital at Caesarea to supervise the keeping of the peace in Jerusalem during the Passover, had taken up residence in the Antonia. Therefore, when Jesus was brought before him to be judged and Pilate wanted to appeal to the people, he had to go out at least to the gateway in order to speak to them. For centuries the arch was believed to be part of the Antonia's gateway until archeologists proved that the Antonia had been practically leveled during the destruction of the city in the year 70. The arch was then found to be part of the triumphal gateway built by Hadrian when, after putting down the Bar Kochba rebellion, he erected his city of Aelia Capitolina in the year 135. Today this triumphal arch makes an impressive background for the altar in the Church of Ecce Homo. But the original gateway to the Antonia was to the rear of the church, and it was here that Pilate put Our Lord before the people, saying, Ecce Homo, "Behold the Man."

At the rear of the church we can also see some of the actual massive rock left there by the Herodian builders as a base for part of the outer wall of the fortress. Beneath this rock are two rooms, the original guardrooms at the entrance of the Antonia.

Descending some stairs to another part of the convent, we come to the most moving part of the remains of the Antonia. Here is the great stone pavement known as the Lithostrotos, or in Hebrew, Gabatha. On some of the flagstones we can see the traces of engravings made by the Roman soldiers for some of the games they played. As one pattern was worn out by the feet of the Roman garrison, another would be out into a nearby stone. One of these engravings, of which there are several different examples, is known as the King Game.

The King Game originated in ancient Rome during the festival honoring the god Saturn. A slave was selected and made king of Rome for the duration of the festival. He was treated with a mixture of honor and contempt and, on the last of the seven days of the feast, he was sacrificed on the altar of Saturn. Later this human sacrifice was done away with and the Saturnalia, as the feast was known, developed into a sort of carnival in which all of Rome was turned upside down. The King Game became a great favorite of the Roman soldiers, and as they were as a group notoriously brutal, it developed into such a cruel sport that they could only play it when they had a condemned criminal as their victim. If they injured him badly, as was often the case, it didn't matter much as he was in any case about to be executed. How Jesus came to be selected as victim of this game the Scriptures do not dwell on; after stating that Pilate, having scourged Our Lord, delivered Him up to be crucified, the Evangelist tells us only that the whole cohort was called together. Why was this done? First of all we must remember that after Pilate condemned Christ to death, a certain time had to elapse before the sentence was carried out: the executioner had to be notified, a cross had to be brought to the Antonia, a guard appointed, and someone put in charge.

Instead of putting Jesus into a guardroom until all was in readiness, the soldiers spread the word that there was a condemned prisoner available for their sport. And how was the game played? The Evangelist tells us quite clearly. They put a royal robe on Him, probably one cast off from the palace. And since it was the cold time of the year, there was probably a great heap of thorn bushes, reeds, and rushes piled in a corner of the courtyard to burn in the bonfires the guard lighted to keep warm while on watch. So, taking some thorn bushes, they plaited them into a crown and put it on the head of Our Saviour. Taking a reed they thrust it into His hand. Thus they had their mock king ready for their game. And since they had heard Pilate refer to Jesus as the king of the Jews, this added further to their cruel mockery. The Roman soldiers, remember, had no reason to mock Our Lord. To them He was merely another local criminal about to be executed. But knowing about their game we can understand why the Roman soldiers mocked Christ. Standing on the Lithostrotos it is very easy for the pilgrim to picture this gross mistreatment of Jesus, and I have seen many whose eyes filled with tears as the scene was described to them.

Adjoining the engravings from the King Game are the remains of the ancient stairway that led from the courtyard up to the actual barracks of the fortress. And farther along the pavement we come to a striated part of the Lithostrotos. This was intended to prevent the soldiers' horses from slipping and was part of the street leading out from the fortress. Our Lord must have walked on these very stones when He was taken out from the Antonia. Is it any wonder one can feel such a presence of Christ here in this place?

Leaving the Ecce Homo convent we proceed along the Via Dolorosa, the sorrowful way, the Way of the Cross. How many groups of pilgrims have traversed this mournful street, taking turns, six or seven at a time, in carrying a cross, happy to be following literally in the footsteps of Jesus! It is a deeply moving religious experience to pass the places where we commemorate the various incidents of that first Way of the Cross.

At the first turning in the road we come to a small chapel, beautifully redecorated by Polish refugees after World War II in thanksgiving for their preservation. The first two stations of the Way of the Cross being at the Moslem boys' school and the Flagellation, both in the Antonia compound, this chapel commemorates the third station, the first fall of Our Saviour under the weight of the cross. The marble statue of Our Lord thus prostrate under the sorrowing eyes of a host of angels is a most touching sight. Just a little farther on is the tiny chapel recalling the fourth station, the meeting of Jesus and His mother. How those two loving hearts must have been pierced by agony at the sight of each other's grief and pain! Then but a short distance on we come to the fifth station. This was at the beginning of the steep climb through the city to the hill of Calvary. Our Lord—exhausted as He was from the Agony at Gethsemane and the trial the night before, the cruel scourging He had received from the Romans, the wearisome journey from the Antonia to the Hasmonean Palace and back, and, above all from the inhuman treatment during the mockery by the soldiers—was physically unable to climb that street with the burden of the cross on His back. Seeing this and fearing He would die before they got Him to Calvary, the soldiers forced a bystander, a certain Simon from Cyrene, to take up the cross and carry it for Jesus. A chapel here commemorates that event. Climbing the steep, stepped street we pass the sixth station honoring the memory of the pious woman we call Veronica, who offered her veil to Our Saviour to wipe His perspiring, bloodstained face. At the top of the street we see the seventh station, the place where He fell a second time. It was near here, commemorated by the eighth station, that He spoke to the women of Jerusalem who shed tears of pity for Him and told them that they should weep, not for Him, but for themselves and for their children. How many of those women and children must have remembered His words amid the fearful siege and destruction of the city some thirty-seven years later. Then we pass the ninth station where He fell yet again.

It happens sometimes that while making the Stations of the Cross, pilgrims are so distracted by the importuning of peddlers and beggars, by the din and crush of shoppers and shopkeepers, and by the chatter and curiosity of tourists that they complain bitterly of all the confusion. I remind them that when Our Blessed Lord carried His cross through these same streets, it was the day of preparation before the Passover and that there was the same noise and confusion. It is now truly as it was then, and the bustle all around should, if anything, help us understand more deeply the turbulent atmosphere in which the first Way of the Cross took place.

Finally we arrive at that holiest of shrines, the Church of the Holy Sepulchre. I can still remember the first time I was privileged to enter this church. I felt a sense of awe, almost of suffocation, that such a favor should be granted me. If only the battered, aged doors by which we enter could speak—what a story they could tell. And, in a way they do speak, for centuries of pilgrims have covered them with carvings. Names are written here that perhaps no longer exist anywhere in the world. Hundreds of crosses are cut into the doors, as indeed they are all over the church, bearing mute witness to pilgrims long dead and long forgotten.

The first thing that greets the visitor upon entering the church is the Stone of Anointing, which commemorates the preparation of the Body of Our Lord for its burial. Ascending the precipitous stairs on our right, we find ourselves on the platform of Calvary. It is fitting that these stairs are steep, for the way to Calvary is ever a difficult one. When Constantine built the first great church on this site, he had the hill of Calvary cut away leaving only a block of stone at the site of the cross. Today the platform upon which we stand is built around that stone. On this spot Our Divine Saviour was stripped of His garment, nailed to the cross, and there He died for each and every one of us. [This is the very spot of our redemption. How can words or pictures convey its sanctity?]

Descending the stairs, we come to that other sacred shrine, the Tomb of Our Lord. There it stands, appearing small and insignificant. How much blood has been spilled, how much pain suffered for possession of this tiny bit of the earth's surface? Entering the Tomb, we kneel amid the flickering light of candles and lamps—Latin, Greek, and Armenian—and bowing our heads, we give thanks for the great grace of being so blessed as to be here. A deep feeling of awe and of peace fills one's very soul. Pilgrim after pilgrim realizes here, perhaps for the first time, the real meaning of Our Lord's suffering and death, the full import of our own redemption.

There are yet other precious places in this most blessed of cities. Toward the southwest of the city, in the part known as Mount Zion, Jesus celebrated the Last Supper. From here He set out for Gethsemane and the beginning of His Passion and Death. Here it was that the Holy Spirit descended upon the poor frightened Apostles and turned them into men of fire and courage, men who went out to face the world and earn a martyr's crown. Here, too, is the traditional tomb of David.

Then there is the present Mosque area, where once stood Solomon's Temple and then the second one so gloriously rebuilt by Herod. Here in the courts of the Temple Jesus was presented as an infant, and here He discoursed with the doctors of the law at the age of twelve, and preached tirelessly during His public life. When we visit this spot we are again overwhelmed by the amount of history that took place here. This was Mount Moriah, where Abraham was about to sacrifice his beloved son, Isaac. Here David and Solomon walked. Here occurred so many great and joyful events but also profound tragedies which must be remembered, the greatest being the terrible end of the Temple in a sea of fire and blood. Here all righteous men shall find sacred hope. Here shall be the beginning of the peace of the world, when "His name shall be called Wonderful...The Prince of Peace."

Looking over the eastern battlements of this area we see far below us the valley of Kidron. If we follow this valley southward but a short distance we arrive at the pool of Siloam, where the blind man received his sight. Then we come to the valley of Hinnom, known as Gehenna, where ancient Jews once lost sight of God and fell into the worship of Baal and Molech. Tradition tells us that it is here, in this forsaken spot, that Judas hanged himself in despair and that here, too, is the potter's field which was bought with the thirty pieces of silver.

Jerusalem, you are a gold and marble city, a domed and crenelated bastion whose walls encircle religion's treasures. Open your gates and reveal your secrets to him who comes to be received into your holy arms. You are a city filled with echoes. Sun-dappled streets vibrate with the sound of a prophet's footsteps. Well-worn stones tell the stories of the hands that touched them. And the voice of the Son of Man reverberates in the translucent air.

Jerusalem that is built to be a city
where people come together in unity;
to which the tribes resort,
the tribes of the Lord,
to give thanks to the Lord Himself,
the bounden duty of Israel.

Psalm 122:3

Jerusalem presides over the kingdom of the faithful and
welcomes all who come to do her honor. Her heritage entices
and mystifies the young. Her holy places stimulate the old and
call them to make the pilgrimage. Islamic, Jewish, and
Christian prophets have walked within her encircling walls
and seekers from each faith now follow those ancient trails.

Moslems from the Arab cities come in uncountable numbers
to visit the place where it is believed Mohammed ascended to
Heaven astride his horse.

Falashas and Sephardim, Moroccans and Ashkenazim,
Yemenites and Hassids—Jews from all the world gather here to
celebrate in the traditional home of their forefathers, to pray
beside the wall of the Temple built for their ancestors.

Christians of all denominations and nationalities pour
through the city's gates every day to worship at the site of their
Saviour's crucifixion and resurrection.

The Wailing Wall, the Dome of the Rock, and the Tomb
of the Holy Sepulchre draw to Jerusalem the prayers of three
great religions. For men of each faith, Jerusalem provides the
certainty that the spirit of their God can be seen upon the earth.

Time passes and the face of a man ages. Yet while the smooth forehead of seven years becomes the wrinkled brow of seventy, the spirit remains untouched. The area of the Temple has lived the lifetime of many men; the face has changed, but the spirit has never grown old. This spirit of tradition reigned in Jerusalem as crown prince. And so, according to the laws of tradition, the baby Jesus was brought to the Temple to be presented to the Lord.

It sometimes happens that a seed of wheat is mixed with seeds of barley. And when the field is planted, amongst all the barley grows something else, a single stalk of wheat. In the midst of all the people who daily crowded the Temple, Jesus was as a stalk of wheat. And His difference was recognized. Simeon the Devout, who had been awaiting the Christ, beheld the child and said to God: "Lord, now lettest Thou Thy servant depart in peace...for my eyes have seen Thy salvation" (Luke 2:29–30). And Anna, the prophetess, saw the baby and raised up her thanks to heaven.

After twelve years the tradition of the faith called Jesus to the Temple once again. He came with His mother and father on a pilgrim journey from Nazareth to celebrate the Passover feast. When the time came to return home, Mary and Joseph set out on the northward road, believing Jesus to be somewhere among the many travelers. But Jesus had remained behind. He sat among the learned men listening to the discussions of the Scriptures and filling the meditative silences with His own speaking and asking. After three days of searching, Mary and Joseph found Him. He knew not that He had been lost.

Many times in His life Jesus came to the Temple. Often He stood upon the steps, beneath the porticoes. He wandered in the courtyards under a hot sun that made the stones warm and the cypress wood smell sweet. That Temple is gone, the structure destroyed. But the smells and the sounds of human creatures pressing in upon a holy place still fill the air, as they must always have filled the air. The shouts of children playing, the colored dresses caught by the breeze, the aged quiet with thoughts of death—these are things of the spirit and they do not change. They are the cords that bind all generations together. This area has passed through the hands of Jews, Christians, and Moslems. Where once rose the massive white stone Temple of Solomon now stands the golden-domed Mosque of Omar. The face has changed but the spirit remains unaltered. And the recollection of all that has happened here clings to the stones like the morning dew.

When men build churches to proclaim their faith they build
Heavenward. By their churches men reveal that they can
reach beyond the material concerns of this world in their
struggle to attain the rewards of Heaven. The skyline of
Jerusalem is a panoply of crosses, domes and towers.

In the fourth century AD, Emperor Constantine declared
Christianity the official religion of the empire. In the name of
Christ and of Constantine, great churches began to be erected.
In each century to follow, money, human life, and years of
labor were dedicated to glorifying the memory of the Son of
Man. And in Jerusalem perhaps the greatest efforts have been
expended, for the city gleams with scores of glorious churches.

When He passed, misery raised its weary head, for He was the sound of relief; despair crawled out from the alleyways, for He was the image of hope, and the afflicted flocked around Him.

There were waters that flowed into Jerusalem which were said to have wondrous qualities. At Bethesda, called "House of Mercy," five porches surrounded a spring whose waters were said to be agitated by the fingertips of angels. The first of the afflicted to wash himself after the angels had stirred the surface would be healed. The Apostle John has written that a cripple, unable to be the first man in the rippling waters, was made whole by Jesus. The pool is no more, but today the Church of St. Anne guards the dry and silent basin.

Another pool, near the Temple, was called Siloam, where now is a village of the same name. Jesus sent a blind man to this spring, and because he who was blind believed in the Word and the water, he was cured. The waters still flow at Siloam and there are those who still believe in its healing touch, as there are those who believe only that it cleanses and cools.

The time of His ministry was short. The end came soon after the beginning. Men live with the certainty only of death, but the Son of Man labored under the prophecy of betrayal, mockery, and crucifixion. In the days left to Him on earth there was still much to be revealed. But time is neither fast nor slow, only steady. Sunday became Thursday and it was the hour to sit at the Last Supper.

The Supper was served and eaten, only to be served over and over again, for the nourishment was in the spirit of the hour. From this single room, in a time when half the world did not exist for the other half, His spirit has reached out, encompassing like the arms of a mother all her children. In each word spoken was the reason for corcerstones of churches, for the prayers of generations, the very seed for century upon century of history to come.

220

*When the meal had been eaten, Jesus and His disciples
went from the Hill of Zion down the steps into the Kidron
Valley. They walked the road which curves past the ruins of
Absalom's tomb and leads to the Mount of Olives and the
garden called Gethsemane.*

The night is long when it is but a prelude to the events of the day to come. It is a time of dark waiting. As a branch heavy with the weight of its own fruit, the Son of Man struggled this final night in the garden. He Who was the true tree was prostrated among the trees. Men forsook Him, but the earth stood fast and comforted Him while His disciples Peter, James, and John, exhausted, slept. Jesus confronted the Fate, the Prophecies, and the Will which bound Him to the Cross.

Men sleep and then sleep forever, taking with them all that they have known. But the land never sleeps. It mirrors for eternity all the destinies it has beheld. The garden of Gethsemane continues to be filled with the anguish of His lonely night there, though the story is revealed in images that are hidden and a voice that is silent. Rarely is the eye of man sharp enough to see what is not visible or his ear fine enough to hear what is not said. And so the story of His Agony and His Resolution awaits always a new discoverer.

In the darkness of the night, Jesus was taken prisoner. Does the ripe fruit of an olive tree cry out, "do not pick me?" When it is time, it must be picked. Jesus did not cry out when it was time, and His captors fed Him into a rocky dungeon. The sun arose and then there was scorning, scourging, pain, and suffering so great that the thought of it today causes suffering anew. In the Antonia fortress He was condemned and then led from the Lithostrotos along the Via Dolorosa to the site of Golgotha, meaning skull. Flesh against wood, blood upon soil; these were the signs that the Mission was at last completed.

A man may chop down the trunk of a tree but in so doing, he does not touch the root which winds and bends in every direction beneath the soil. So when men tried to destroy Jesus, they failed, for they could not destroy the root. When He came, the Apostle John tells us, "the Word was made flesh…" When He left the earth, He left behind Him that Word which endures forever, a root which was indeed made stronger by His presence for those few short years among men.

From the land where He lived rises up the Message: "Forgive the unforgivable, Pity the pitiless, Be merciful to the merciless And love the unlovable."

Men are forgetful creatures, often too busy with the present to remember the past. Walking along the Via Dolorosa, traveling the Way of the Cross, is a means of setting aside Today and renewing the memory of Then.

At 3:00 PM a group of pilgrims gathers to follow the route taken by Jesus as He bore the cross to Golgotha. The road is commonly called the Via Dolorosa, meaning "sorrowful way." They stand at the Antonia Gateway and remember that here Jesus was condemned to death. This is the First Station of the Way of the Cross. The great gates, wide enough for a horse and chariot, open slowly and the pilgrims pass through. In the company of two thieves, Jesus received the cross as He stepped beyond these gates. The Second Station. The Via Dolorosa moves westward. Many pilgrims walk barefoot, feeling the hard stone beneath their feet. The sounds of motors and radios fade into insignificance. The cross that Jesus carried was heavy, a cruel burden, and the weight of it caused Him to fall to the ground. The Third Station. The sadness of the journey deepens, becomes as tangible as the walls that line the road. In their hands, many pilgrims hold the Apostles' accounts of these final hours, their lips silently forming the written words.

The Via Dolorosa turns southward and dips into a valley. At the place where the road turns, Mary, mother of Jesus, stood amongst the crowd and watched her martyred son struggle past. The Fourth Station. The road resumes its westward course. At the corner here, Simon of Cyrene was seized by Roman guards and ordered to bear the cross that Jesus could no longer support. The Fifth Station. The pilgrim need not dismiss the shouts of children playing, nor disregard the odors of cooking and dung, for such sounds and odors assailed Him as He journeyed to Golgotha.

The Via Dolorosa continues, crawling upwards, out of the valley. It is said that here where the road begins to ascend, a woman stepped forward and wiped the sweat from Jesus' brow. The Sixth Station. The road extends to the crest of the incline and here Jesus fell for the second time. The Seventh Station. Where the Via Dolorosa meets Francis Street, it is written, Jesus slowed His pace and begged the onlookers to weep not for Him but for themselves and their children. The Eighth Station. A convent is built across the road, and the Via Dolorosa changes its direction. Pilgrims pass amidst the hubbub of the marketplace and mount a flight of steps. Here Jesus fell for the third time. The Ninth Station. The road ends. Jesus climbed the hill upon which He was crucified. The pilgrim reaches the Tomb of the Holy Sepulchre. The remaining stations of the cross are within the church.

Daily, the Via Dolorosa is washed by tears, the stones rubbed smooth by pilgrims' feet. For there is no better way to remember the drama and anguish of the hour than to live that hour once again.

Four times in a year one season ends only to give way to the new, for the calendar of months is a series of fresh beginnings. Jesus was crucified on Calvary and buried in the nearby tomb of Joseph of Arimathea. As spring is an annual resurrection, so is He life's eternal spring. For the Apostles have written that though He was dead on Friday, He arose on Sunday. He passed out through the doors of the world of the body and in through the gates of the kingdom of the spirit.

It is said in the third Gospel about the blessed resurrection morning when the women went early to the tomb: "And they found the stone rolled away from the sepulchre. And they entered in, and found not the body of the Lord Jesus." But angels appeared and said, "Why seek ye the living among the dead? He is not here, but is risen: remember how He spake unto you when He was yet in Galilee…" (Luke 24 : 2–6).

The Church of the Resurrection includes what all believe is the site of Golgotha and the Tomb. It is a maze of cool caverns and shining golden altars. It is a massive house for the spirit of renewal, for within its walls darkness becomes light, struggle becomes peace, and death becomes life again and again.

231

To the observant the world offers many signs of the future. In a thick black cloud is a forewarning of rain. A flower growing in the winter chill speaks of spring. In the green leaf which sprouts from a barren twig is promise of coming life.

Jerusalem, rising splendid and monumental from the naked hill, was also a harbinger. When Jesus stood upon a distant mound His own destiny was foretold in the skyline of the city, and He revealed to His disciples all that would befall Him. They could not know the truth that was made manifest to Him by the sight of Jerusalem, nor could He do other than recognize the sign.

EPILOGUE

"And it is my prayer that your love may abound more and more, with knowledge and all discernment, so that you may approve what is excellent..."
(Philippians 1:9–10)

It may be that some readers, having laid aside this book, will experience, as some do who visit the Holy Land, a sense of disillusionment. Quite apart from the merits of this volume, it is certain that although the Holy Places respond to the state of mind of the visitor, they reveal their message unwillingly and demand a special attention to the power of the Spirit.

As we contemplate Gospel sites today, we find many which do not correspond exactly either to those that existed at the time of Christ or to those we have visualized when reading the familiar stories. But, as elsewhere, time has not passed in vain in the Holy Land, and the reality, albeit less beautiful, has positive value.

After 2,000 years Nazareth is still only a small town, as are so many others in the Holy Land; the place where Christ was born is but a cave; the garden of Gethsemane lies within only a few hundred square meters of earth; the Via Dolorosa can be traversed in a few minutes; Calvary is but a small elevation; and the Holy Sepulchre must be sought through oriental bazaars and lanes, hidden amid a haphazard conglomeration of buildings. Moreover, due to an infinity of historical and local vicissitudes, some places sanctified by the earthly presence of Christ and very dear to the piety of Christians are in a state of almost total disrepair. Understandably, a spirit which is unprepared can hardly refrain from exclaiming: "But is all here?" Yes, it is all here. For the "Fifth Gospel" cannot belie all that has been taught us by the other Four. Christianity is above all else a lesson in spiritual divesting, a teaching of humility and abasement; Divinity loves to shield itself with humble veils.

Some of our contemporaries, as yet preoccupied with the creation of an atmosphere and with observing a ceremony for everything, would wish for something different—just like many of Jesus' contemporaries who, to recognize the Messiah, would have had to have a more solemn setting—something, in short, more in keeping with the theophany of which the books of the Old Testament speak. They fail to notice that fixed formulas, beaten tracks, studied and pre-established plans have always constituted an obstacle to divine communications.

Souls profoundly sensitive to the voice of the Spirit know only too well that the Holy Land can offer us naught but a vision of poor things connected with Jesus, the Saviour of the humble and the weak.

In its vision of the Holy Places The Fifth Gospel has aspired to render better known the sole dimension of the world and of history: the incarnation of God.

All those who strive sincerely for the upbuilding of the "Terrestrial City" should keep this in sight: If, as is said today, life must incarnate itself in temporal structures, then we must absolutely keep in view this 2,000-year-old dimension.

The verbal delirium and pompous vocabulary of the advocates of man and the world of today have no meaning for one who understands the message transmitted to us by the Holy Places. The fact that "the Word was made flesh and pitched his tent among us" (John 1:14) infuses us with a new sympathy for humanity and for the world and reveals to us that love for man and the world is only the first step in the ascent toward a supreme and transcendent end, toward the cause of all love.

He who traverses the stages of the life of Christ right up to Calvary must be persuaded that in life one does not strive to return wreathed with garlands, amid universal recognition, amid smiles and applause. The "Fifth Gospel"—exactly like the Four written by Matthew, Mark, Luke, and John—gives us the key to the just explanation of suffering: "It was necessary that the Christ should suffer that He might enter into His glory" (Luke 24:26). But this is a hard lesson, and how could anyone accept it? (John 6:61). Yet to place a limit to the Christian lesson, be it ever so hard, means living in conflict with the presence of God. And if, to suppose the absurd, such an effort should succeed, we will then feel the tragedy of the words of Flaubert: "There is no longer Christianity. And in recompense what is there? Railways, chemistry, mathematics. Yes, the body is better, the flesh suffers less, but the heart ever bleeds."

The reader of The Fifth Gospel may have remarked that the streets of the villages and towns of the Holy Land have nothing very extraordinary about them; they are like those of our villages and towns, just as the paths through those fields are not much different from the paths through our fields. Yet only those contemplated in this volume have been traversed by Christ. On those only took place the encounters recorded in the Gospels: Jesus with the lake fishermen, with the Magdalen, with Zacchaeus, with the man born blind, with the adulteress, with the Samaritan woman, and with the paralytic.

A personal and serious encounter with Jesus of Nazareth necessarily produces an interior crisis, a crisis which often changes the course of life and which, if positively adopted, is always beneficial.

The lake fishermen became apostles, fishers of men; Magdalen changed her love; Zacchaeus acquired a profound social sensibility; the man born blind was given his sight and granted faith in the "Son of Man;" the Samaritan woman received the living water which quenches all thirst; the adulteress was saved from imminent stoning and taught fidelity to the conjugal bond; and the paralytic had health of body together with remission of his sins.

Perhaps the reader going through the pages of The Fifth Gospel and contemplating the landscape of the Holy Land feels he has found himself in a country with which he was already acquainted and which in some way belonged to him. This is also true, for how mingled is the Holy Land with our childhood memories.

In the Holy Land everyone feels at home.

The Holy Land leads to a more complete knowledge of Christ. Even though the past of Jesus Christ is relived in its entirety in the presence of His Resurrection, it is important to know all that relates to the earthly life of Jesus. For the life of Jesus was lived in a fixed time and place.

The Holy Land has interest for every Christian because every Christian is involved in the action of Christ.

Faith does not ask the Christian to suppress the historical facts of Christ. It obliges him, rather, to follow without pause the path traced by the Evangelists. To understand that mystery it is necessary to refer continually to the historical event of Jesus so as not to be lost in imagination.

Christ is with us always even to the end of the world (Matthew 28:10), and we adhere to this promise of Jesus, even though the history has not yet finished. It was He Who said: "Do not be afraid, it is I, the First and Last. I am the Living One. I was dead and now I am to live for ever and ever" (Revelation 1:17-18).

Fr. Ignazio Mancini, OFM

A Guide for Pilgrims

JERUSALEM

In suggesting these sites, we have started at St. Stephen's Gate, as most pilgrimage tours do, and listed the places to be visited in the order in which one comes upon them. After the Church of the Holy Sepulchre, we have listed other interesting sites in the city and then areas near Jerusalem.

St. Anne's Church One of the finest Crusader churches in the Holy Land, it marks the place where, according to ancient tradition, Mary the mother of Jesus was born. In the church compound the remains of the great pool of Bethesda have been excavated. It was here that Jesus cured the paralytic who had been ill for thirty-eight years.

The Convent of the Flagellation The Franciscan School of Biblical Studies stands on part of the Antonia fortress. This fortress was built by Herod the Great and named after his friend, Mark Anthony. Here Pilate took up residence on the first Good Friday. It was here that Jesus was condemned and given the cross He was to carry to Golgotha. Those two spots are the first two stations of the Way of the Cross. The scourging of Our Lord took place here and the Chapel of the Flagellation commemorates that event.

Convent of the Sisters of Sion (Church of the Ecce Homo) This convent is also built over the ruins of the Antonia. Here one sees part of the triumphal arch erected by the Emperor Hadrian in A.D. 135. Here also is the Lithostrotos, or Gabatha, the great stone-paved courtyard of the Antonia, where the Roman soldiers played their cruel game of mockery with Jesus. Several remains of this ancient game can still be seen cut into the pavement. A striated part of the pavement is also important, as it was on these stones that Jesus trod when He left the Antonia to begin His way to Calvary.

Via Dolorosa The sorrowful Way of the Cross commemorating the events that took place on that sad journey:

Station 3 The first fall of Jesus beneath the Cross. This lovely small chapel was redecorated by Polish refugees after World War II in thanksgiving for their preservation. It is open every day.

Station 4 Also redecorated by the Polish refugees, it commemorates the meeting of Jesus and His mother while He was carrying the cross. It is open during the public Way of the Cross every Friday.

Station 5 From this point Jesus, more dead than alive, had to begin the steep climb to Golgotha. His guard, fearing He might die before reaching Golgotha, forced a bystander, Simon of Cyrene, to carry the Cross in His place. The chapel is open during the public Way of the Cross.

Station 6 This commemorates the pious woman we call Veronica, who, in compassion, presented her veil to Jesus to wipe His face. To enter, ring the bell on the door.

Station 7 Here Jesus fell a second time under the Cross. The chapel is open during public Stations on Friday.

Station 8 At this place Jesus spoke with the weeping women and made reference to the coming destruction of the city. The only sign of the station is a small cross cut into the wall of the Greek monastery.

Station 9 Here was the third fall of Jesus under the weight of the Cross. It is marked by a pillar set into the wall at the entrance to the Coptic Orthodox Patriarchate. Adjoining is the interesting Ethiopian Coptic community of monks who have their dwellings on the roof of the Chapel of St. Helena in the Holy Sepulchre.

The Basilica of the Holy Sepulchre This church is the work of the Crusaders in the twelfth century. Today it is owned by the Roman Catholics (known as the Latins in the Holy Land), by the Greek Orthodox, and the Armenian Orthodox. On entering the church, the pilgrim ascends the steep stairway to his right and finds himself on the platform of Calvary, or Golgotha. The right side with the mosaic ceiling belongs to the Latins, the other side with the painted ceiling, to the Greeks. On the Latin side we come to the tenth and eleventh stations where Jesus was stripped of His garments and nailed to the cross. The twelfth station where He died on the cross is beneath the Greek altar. The altar to the right is the thirteenth station where He was taken down from the cross and placed in the arms of His mother. Descending the stairs we come to the Stone of Anointing. After the Crucifixion the Body of Our Lord was prepared for burial; the exact spot where this took place is not known, but it is commemorated by this stone. Going a little farther we come to the Sepulchre itself. The tomb of Our Lord was originally cut from the side of a hill. Constantine, who ordered the construction of the first great church, had the hill cut away leaving the bare walls of the tomb which were then enclosed in a shrine. He also had the hill of Golgotha cut away leaving only a block of stone. All subsequent churches have been built on the great circular cut made by Constantine.

Russian Excavations Some remains of the triumphal arch of Hadrian that led into the Forum were unearthed here, as well as remains of the city wall from Jesus' time and a city gate.

Mount Zion The great Church of the Dormition Abbey is one of the landmarks of the city of Jerusalem. It was built by Kaiser Wilhelm II and marks the traditional place where Mary fell into her final sleep. The Latin word *dormitio* means sleep.

Nearby is the Upper Room. When the first Judeo-Christians returned to Jerusalem after its destruction, they sought out the site of the Last Supper and the Descent of the Holy Spirit and built a small house-church there. When the Byzantines came in the fourth century they built a great basilica here which was destroyed in the seventh century. The Crusaders built another church on the foundations of the Byzantine, and this, in turn, was destroyed on their expulsion, save for a transept chapel which commemorated the actual site of the Upper Room and stood, according to a twelfth-century tradition, over the Tomb of King David.

Cathedral of St. James (Armenian Orthodox Patriarchate) The twelfth-century church contains many rich spiritual and artistic treasures.

St. Stephen's Church (Ecole Biblique) This Dominican basilica stands upon the site of the basilica erected by the Empress Eudoxia in the fifth century.

MOUNT OF OLIVES

Chapel of the Ascension The small, domed chapel (Crusader) is all that is left of the great Byzantine and Crusader structures that stood on this site commemorating the Ascension of Our Lord into heaven.

Pater Noster Church Constantine erected here the great Basilica of the Eleona. It marked the site where Jesus taught the Apostles "many mysteries" and also the "Our Father." The present church and convent were built for the Carmelite nuns by the French Princess de la Tour d'Auvergne, Duchess of Bouillon.

Chapel of Dominus Flevit The modern chapel was built on the foundations of Byzantine and Crusader churches, at the site where Jesus wept over Jerusalem and foretold its complete destruction.

Gethsemane The great basilica, considered by many the most beautiful in the Holy Land, commemorates the Agony in the Garden, as did its Byzantine and Crusader predecessors. Inside the church one sees the rock upon which, according to most ancient tradition, Jesus suffered His Agony. Nearby is the grotto of Gethsemane. The word Gethsemane comes from two Hebrew words meaning "oil press." The remains of an ancient oil press were in fact discovered in the grotto. Tradition has it that the Apostles waited here for Jesus and that it was at the mouth of this grotto that He was betrayed by Judas.

Tomb of Mary Near the Grotto is the Crusader church covering the Byzantine remains over the traditional tomb of the Virgin Mary.

THE KIDRON VALLEY

The Pinnacle of the Temple This was the southwest corner of the Temple compound and the scene of the second temptation of Jesus by the devil. It was from here that the first bishop of Jerusalem, James the Lesser, was thrown to his death.

The Spring of Gihon The ancient source of Jerusalem's water supply, the spring is also the beginning of the famous tunnel of Hezekiah which brought this water to the pool of Siloam, the scene of the curing of the blind man.

Haceldama This is the "Field of Blood," which was purchased with the thirty pieces of silver and used as a burial place for strangers. It is also the legendary place where Judas committed suicide.

St. Peter in Gallicantu Church Here Peter's triple denial of Our Lord is commemorated. Nearby one sees part of the ancient stepped street used by Our Lord when He went from the Upper Room to Gethsemane.

Mount Moriah According to tradition Abraham brought Isaac to Mount Moriah to offer him up in sacrifice. Here was the threshing floor purchased by David in order to build the Temple, actually erected by his son Solomon. The second Temple stood on this same site, and it is here that Jesus was presented as a babe. Here He was found discussing the Law with the doctors of the Law at the age of twelve. Here He so often taught. Today the great rock is crowned by the exquisitely beautiful Mosque of the Dome of the Rock.

Western Wall For centuries the Jews wept over the destruction of the Temple at this remaining portion of the great retaining wall of the Temple area built by Herod the Great. Thus it became known as the Wailing Wall.

Bethphage This was once the site of the village of this name on the eastern slopes of the Mount of Olives. Here it was that Our Lord began His triumphal entry into Jerusalem on the first Palm Sunday.

Bethany This was the home of Jesus' friends, Mary, Martha, and Lazarus, and the scene of the raising of Lazarus from the dead.

BETHLEHEM

The Basilica of the Nativity In the basilica is the grotto where Our Lord was born. The great church built here by Constantine was destroyed during the Samaritan revolt in 529. The Emperor Justinian had it rebuilt the following year. The front of the church was covered by a great mosaic depicting the three Wise Men in the garb of the ancient Persian Magi. In the seventh century when the Persian hordes destroyed all the Christian shrines, they spared this church out of superstitious fear of the Magi depicted on the façade. There are other shrines here, too, including those commemorating St. Jerome, who spent the latter part of his life, here, and the Holy Innocents.

The Shepherds' Field A cave and a modern chapel mark the probable place where the shepherds were keeping watch that first Christmas night.

The Milk Grotto An ancient legend states that while feeding the Infant Jesus, Mary let some drops of her milk spill on the ground and the rocks turned pure white.

EIN KEREM

Church of the Visitation The exquisite chapel commemorates the place where Mary visited her cousin Elizabeth after the Annunciation and spent three months caring for her.

Church of St. John This church marks the place where, since earliest times, it has been believed that the birth of John the Baptist took place.

EMMAUS

On the first Easter Sunday two of Our Lord's disciples were returning to their village from Jerusalem. Jesus joined them, but they were prevented from recognizing Him. As they walked along He explained the Scriptures to them and showed them how these had been fulfilled in the Life and Death of Jesus. Arriving at their home, they persuaded Jesus to remain with them and share their evening meal. When He broke the bread, they recognized Him "in the breaking of the bread." Emmaus is the traditional site of this event. The present church is built upon the remains of the Crusader shrine. There are also remains of Crusader houses, as well as a fragment of an ancient Roman road.

INN OF THE GOOD SAMARITAN

Halfway along the road from Jerusalem to Jericho are the remains of a Turkish Khan. All through history there has been an inn at this spot. Tradition holds that this is the inn mentioned in the parable of the Good Samaritan. On the opposite hill one can see the remains of a Crusader fort.

JERICHO

As far as is known to archeologists today, Jericho is the oldest city on earth. Two events recorded in the New Testament occurred here. The first was that of Zacchaeus, the tax collector, who climbed the sycamore tree the better to see Jesus as He passed. The second was the curing of blind Bartimeus. Here, too, is the Mount of Temptation where the first and third temptations of Jesus are said to have taken place.

DEAD SEA

A few miles to the south of Jericho lies the Dead Sea, the lowest spot on the face of the earth.

QUMRAN

This was the great center where the community of the Essenes had their home. In the first century A.D. upon the advance of the Roman armies during the great revolt against Rome, the Essenes quickly hid their precious library in the nearby caves. As the members of the community were all massacred, the scrolls remained undiscovered until our own century. These are the famous Dead Sea Scrolls.

NAZARETH

The town where Jesus spent so many years of His life contains many important sites. The principal ones are:

The Basilica of the Annunciation The large modern church contains the remains of Crusader, Byzantine, and Judeo-Christian shrines. In the lower church one sees the Holy Grotto where the Annunciation took place and where the Word was made Flesh.

Church of St. Joseph This covers what is traditionally believed to have been the home of the Holy Family upon their return from Egypt. A Byzantine baptismal font can still be seen in the lower church.

Mary's Well This ancient fountain lies beneath the Greek Orthodox Church. It was the source of the ancient town's water supply.

The Synagogue It is in the center of the old town. At the present Greek Catholic Church, Jesus taught His fellow townsmen and was rejected by them.

The Hill of Precipitation South of the town is the traditional spot where His fellow townsmen brought Jesus in order to cast Him down.

CANA

The small red-domed Franciscan church marks the traditional spot of the first miracle of Jesus.

SEA OF GALILEE

This is the scene of most of the Public Life of Our Lord. The Jordan River flows into it at the northern end and out of its southern end. The sea has many moods, from peaceful serenity to violent storms. The main points of interest in the area are:

Jordan River The pilgrim can best enjoy it at the southern end of the lake as the river flows out toward the Dead Sea.

Capernaum, Tabgha, and the Mount of Beatitudes are all at the northern end of the Sea of Galilee.

Capernaum Here was Jesus' chosen home for His public ministry. He worked many of His miracles in Capernaum. He cured Peter's mother-in-law, the man with the withered hand, the paralytic who had to be let down through the roof, the woman with the issue of blood, the servant of the centurion, and He raised Jairus' daughter from the dead. In the synagogue at Capernaum He cured the possessed man and later, in the same synagogue, He promised to give His own Flesh to be man's spiritual food. It was here that Matthew was called, here that He asked Peter to catch the fish and take from its mouth the coin to pay the Temple tax. Today one can see the ruins of a later synagogue and the Byzantine church built over the remains of Peter's house.

Tabgha Three important sites are in this area:

The Chapel of the Primacy It marks the spot where Our Lord appeared to the Apostles after His Resurrection and told Peter to feed His lambs and His sheep.

The Church of the Loaves and Fishes It commemorates the first multiplication of loaves and fishes. The mosaics seen in the Benedictine church date from the fourth century.

Chapel of the Sermon on the Mount The Byzantine ruins mark the traditional place where Jesus preached the sermon. They are across from the small restaurant at Tabgha.

The Mount of the Beatitudes The chapel commemorates the Sermon on the Mount, although it was preached at the foot of the hill. Here Jesus spent the night in prayer with His disciples before choosing the twelve as His Apostles the following morning and descending the mountain to preach His wonderful Sermon to the people.

Magdala At the northwest end of the Sea of Galilee is the site of the small town which was the home of Mary the Magdalen.

Chorazin Two miles north of Capernaum is the site of one of the three towns cursed by Our Lord for refusing to accept His teachings. The ruins of an ancient synagogue can be visited here.

MOUNT TABOR

This is the traditional "mountain set apart" to which Our Lord took Peter, James, and John and was transfigured before them. A great modern basilica stands on the ruins of the Byzantine and the Crusader churches. In the Old Testament Mount Tabor is connected with the prophetess Deborah.

NAIN

A small church commemorates the miracle of the raising of the widow's son.

HAIFA

High above the town is Mount Carmel, the birthplace of the Carmelite Order. The beautiful Church of Stella Maris contains the famous Image of Our Lady of Mount Carmel.

JAFFA

This city goes back to the most ancient times. Greek mythology says that Andromeda was saved from the sea monster on the rocks below the town. The Old Testament pointed it out as the town from which Jonah set sail. It was here that Peter raised Tabitha from the dead. Here, too, Peter was ordered to accept the Gentiles into the church and the first Gentile, the Centurion Cornelius, was baptized.

HEBRON

Here are the tombs of the Patriarchs Abraham, Isaac, and Jacob and their wives. The great walls surrounding the Cave of Machpelah date back to Herod the Great.

MEGIDDO

One of the great cities of antiquity, it is first mentioned in the thirteenth century B.C. in the records of Thutmose III in his temple in Upper Egypt, where the battle he waged against Megiddo is described in detail. However, it is even more ancient. It was destroyed by Joshua. Among the many interesting archeological finds, one can see the great "stables of Solomon." From the words Har Megiddo ("the hill of Megiddo") we have the word Armageddon, the place legend tells us the last great battle between the forces of good and evil will be fought.

HATZOR

Another great city of antiquity, it was also among those destroyed by Joshua and rebuilt by Solomon.

MASSADA

Herod the Great built an enormous fortress on the lofty rock. It was here that after the destruction of Jerusalem the Zealots held out for three years against the might of Rome. Finally, rather than fall into the hands of the Romans, the entire garrison with their families committed suicide.

EIN GEDI

This luxuriant oasis on the shores of the Dead Sea is one of the great beauty spots of the country. David hid here from Saul's anger. Not far from Ein Gedi, Professor Yigael Yadin discovered the important Bar Kochba finds.

ACRE

This town was mentioned in ancient Egyptian texts. After the fall of the Crusader Kingdom of Jerusalem, Acre held out for nearly another hundred years. Today the rich Crusader and Moslem remains make it a fascinating place for the visitor.

CAESAREA

The Roman capital of Palestine for some five hundred years, this city was built by Herod the Great and named after Augustus Caesar. There are many Roman ruins here, as well as the walls and part of the Crusader town.

BEERSHEBA

This was the southernmost town in Biblical times. Its origins go far back into the mists of antiquity. The ancient well traditionally connected with Abraham is still pointed out.

This cross is an adaptation from the "Cosmic Cross"
wich is cut in the stone of a 6th century
church in Umm el-Jamal. It symbolizes,
in its vertical arm, the link of sky to earth
and, in its horizontal arm, the link that
embraces all parts of the world.